About the Author

Dave Hall was born in Exeter, England, and educated in H.M. Forces schools around the world due to his father being in the military. He now lives in Newcastle-upon-Tyne with his wife Yvonne. They built a property portfolio of 20 properties in two years with virtually no money. They run a successful lettings and property management company in County Durham.

Dave's passion is helping landlords and with this in mind he set up a free tenant-vetting website for landlords to help them avoid dodgy tenants. (www.landlordsbestfriend.co.uk)

Having dealt with hundreds of landlords over the years, he feels that there is a real lack of information out there for novice landlords. The idea behind this book is to tell them how it *really* is, so they don't make the same mistakes he did.

It tells you his story so far in his own words from being a barman in Benidorm to owning a seven-figure property portfolio.

DAVE HALL

WHO'D BE A LANDLORD?

Matador
9 Priory Business Park
Kibworth Beauchamp
Leicestershire LE8 0RX, UK
Tel: (+44) 116 279 2299
Fax: (+44) 116 279 2277
Email: books@troubador.co.uk
Web: www.troubador.co.uk/matador

ISBN 978 1780885 032

British Library Cataloguing in Publication Data.
A catalogue record for this book is available from the British Library.

Typeset in 11pt Minion Pro by Troubador Publishing Ltd, Leicester, UK

Matador is an imprint of Troubador Publishing Ltd

Printed and bound in the UK by TJ International, Padstow, Cornwall

This book is dedicated to my mum and dad, who both sadly died of cancer. Without them I wouldn't be here. It is also dedicated to my gorgeous wife Yvonne, without whom I wouldn't have had the stories to tell about our journey as husband and wife, our successes and failures in property and what we have achieved together. It is a story about our life together so far, our trials and tribulations in the property game and the tenants who have ripped us off, wrecked some of our properties and laughed at the government who decided it would be a good idea to pay the tenants their housing benefit instead of the landlords – idiots!

Do not even consider buying your first buy-to-let property until you have read this book. Unlike most other books on buy-to-let, mine will give you an insight into this weird and wonderful world. If it scares you, great! If it inspires you, great! If it puts you off, great!

I have written it to open your eyes to the pitfalls as well as the positives of this industry so you don't go in blind.

Buy-to-let is not for everybody and some people are just not cut out for it. Everything in this book is based on actual events and our own experiences in this industry. Names of individuals have been changed to protect their identity, but believe me, you couldn't make some of it up. It's factual, not fictional!

If you still want to get into buy-to-let after reading this book then at least you will be armed with the knowledge of how it is in reality. Enjoy it, and good luck!

Table of Contents

Chapter 1

The Millennium – A New Beginning

Where do I start? If there has ever been a way to make money and lose money, then being a landlord has to be one of the things you can do to become a millionaire or go bankrupt.

Yes, being a landlord, it has been said by many, is not for the faint-hearted!

So what made me decide that property was the way forward, to a secure future?

In the wake of my life, jumping around from job to job, with frozen pension funds here and there, and a wife whose trustees had decided to spend her final salary pension fund, I decided that there has got to be a better place to invest money and get a better return. I had sold a couple of properties and made a profit before, but thought nothing of it at the time. I thought that the timing must have just been right or I was just lucky. But luck, as I have found out, plays only a very small part in making money from property.

I won't bore you with my life story but what I will tell you is that I am from a working class background. My mum was a chef and my dad served twenty-two years in the army. We spent our lives travelling the world as Dad had a posting every two to three years to somewhere in the world. So we never owned a property as a family until my Dad retired in 1979. Mum and Dad bought a house which was to become our home for the next thirty years for

£14,000. The one and only property they ever owned. I always remember Mum telling me the story about Dad asking her where they were going to live when they got out of the army. Mum said, 'Well I'm going to live in Newcastle, so you can please yourself.' Dad was from Portsmouth and decided that he didn't want to live there. So Newcastle it was. He got his Geordie passport and that was where we would live!

So the year was 2000 – the millennium – a new beginning!
I had left Germany where I had worked for the previous five years as a car salesman, selling to Her Majesty's Armed Forces and the American Armed Forces. Being an ex-squaddie myself it was a great job for me as I knew the jargon and the way of life and got to see a lot of old army mates. An interesting but sometimes boring job selling cars to our lads and lasses in green kit. Oh, sorry, and blue kit – we sold to the air force as well. When they came back from whatever tour of duty they had been on they had a few quid in the bank. Obviously there's nowhere to spend it when you're fighting the Bosnians apart from a famous burger bar, if you were lucky enough to be stationed near the Americans. They are treated like superstars compared to our boys and girls on the front line... don't even get me started on that one. Anyway, getting back to selling cars to the ones who were lucky enough to make it back from the war zones. I sold a car to a young girl who was only eighteen years old. She had been to a war zone – Bosnia – and she was excited at the prospect of taking delivery of her first car. We had to order it and it would take about six weeks to arrive. I can remember her little face and how excited she was. Blonde hair, fresh complexion, good looking, and as fit as a butcher's dog. She was in her corps hockey team and she was going to the UK that weekend to play in a tournament. She ordered a blue Rover 200 series

hatchback, a 3-door. It was metallic paint and had a CD player. In her words, it was mint! After the £100 deposit was paid and the finance forms were signed, she was away. As she left my portable showroom, I smiled and thought, that's what it's all about. Eighteen, footloose and fancy free. She had a steady job, had been on R&R (rest and recuperation) and was going away with her mates for a game of hockey and a few glasses of beer or wine, or whatever they drink at that age. Nice girl.

I arrived for work at 9 am sharp. It was a sunny day and I could see a couple of soldiers waiting by my portable showroom for me to open. Happy days, I thought, more punters, it should be a great start to the week. They must be keen to buy a car to be there at that time of the day. I greeted them in the usual way, and noticed that they weren't very friendly. Well, not unfriendly, but not a lot of banter like the usual lads that turn up, full of beans, to buy a new car. 'Could we have a word about a car you sold last week?' one of them chirped up. Here we go, I thought, one of them young lads from last week has changed his mind, and has got his boss to come and give me some sob story about him not being able to afford it and could he cancel his order. 'What's the problem?' I asked. 'Well,' he said, 'you sold a car to a young private last week, her name was Sally, blonde hair…' I cut him off. 'It was last Thursday and she was over the moon with it,' I said. 'She has only ordered it but it won't be here for a few weeks,' I added. 'You will have to cancel the order,' he said. 'Why?' I asked. 'Because she was involved in a terrible accident at the weekend. She was with the hockey team and they pulled over in the minibus to have a pee. Some of the girls did anyway; Sally didn't need to go and stayed on the bus. A foreign lorry driver fell asleep at the wheel of his juggernaut and ploughed straight into the bus, killing Sally and another girl instantly by all accounts. So we went through all of her things and found the order for this car. Is there any way you can cancel the order?' 'Obviously, that's no problem, I'll take care of it,' I said. They left my little office and it took me a few minutes to digest what they had just said. I don't mind admitting that I had a few tears in my eyes. I had only just met the girl last week and now her parents and family were going to have to bury her. She survived a warzone and some lorry driver has taken her life, because he didn't pull over and get some sleep. Unbelievable, but true.

The point of me telling you that little story is this: nothing is guaranteed in life. You speculate to accumulate, and as previously stated, property isn't for the faint-hearted. You can plan for the future and you can live for now. My advice to you is this: live life to the full and put a bit away for a rainy day. If you don't enjoy what you are doing – stop doing it and find something else to do. I left Germany shortly after that incident!

I had no job, no wife or girlfriend to answer to and no idea what I was going to do next for a living. I had no bills but had some savings. I went back to my mum's to live. If I ever get asked, when did Princess Diana die? I always know the answer. September 1997. Dad died on the 3rd December 1997 so I think Mum was glad to have me home for a bit. She looked after me as she always did and asked the question that all mothers would... 'What are you going to do now?' So I told her. 'I'm off to Benidorm, Mum!' It had previously been a holiday destination of mine and I thought it was as good a place as any to go as I knew the town pretty well and a few of the bar owners. I packed a case and took £2,000 spending money. I thought I would go for a sabbatical, I told her. A few months off to clear my head and decide what I was going to do with my life. She always supported me, my mum. No matter what I did, she was always there for me. She said she would come and visit when I got myself sorted, which she did.

Now, there is only so much beach time that I can do. Every day, going down to the beach and having a look at all the topless women sunbathing. Home for a shower and out on the drink. Home after a kebab or a burger at John & Joseph's and back to my hotel. I thought, my money is going to run out at this rate and I had better get a little job if I want to stay here a bit longer. It was January and all the bars were pretty quiet. I asked around every day in different pubs and clubs if they had any bar work, and got the same answer at all of them... 'It's quiet at the moment, come back in April when we get a bit busier.' Now I'm no shirker, and had a decision to make. Go back home to Mum's and come back in April or get some other job. I was in a bar contemplating this very decision when a Dutch guy called Hans asked me if I was looking for work. We got chatting and he said he would give me a start if I wanted it. He was a general builder-cum-odd-job man, and had a few clients who he did work for. He even watered rich people's gardens up in the hills near Benidorm. So I told him I was up for anything he could offer. Cash in hand at the end of every day and that was fine with me.

Because of the heat of the day, we would start every day at 6.30 am. We would meet at 6 am at the local "workers café" for a croissant and a cappuccino, before jumping in his van and heading off to wherever.

He was a clever guy and had taught himself Spanish. He said he just learnt about four words per day until he could string sentences together, and then learnt the numbers and grammar, and hey presto he could speak Spanish! Yeah, whatever, I thought. Either way, he could speak it fluently and had some good crack with the locals, so I knew he could speak it pretty well, even if he wasn't fluent.

Anyway, he not only spoke Spanish but he had a few contacts and he managed to get me an apartment close to town, which was affordable on my wages. He helped me open a bank account and all of a sudden I had a life again, with a purpose to get up in the morning, and somewhere to live. Instead of sitting in bars on my own like Billy-No-Mates, with holidaymakers looking at me like I was some saddo on holiday on my own – which I was!

I worked with Hans until about April. It was hard work labouring in the heat, but I was losing weight and getting a bit fitter, after five years of sitting on my backside selling cars. My new employer said he would just be watering gardens over the summer months and would be back on the building game in about October if I needed any work. We shook hands and went our separate ways. He was a great bloke Hans, I never saw him again.

I managed to get myself a job at the now infamous Black Chicken, as featured on the television. It was a tiny little bar that sold alcohol, tea, coffee and the odd dodgy toasty.

I met Jimmy and Karen, two more Dutch people who – yes, you guessed it – spoke fluent Spanish! Karen worked behind the bar with me and Jimmy was a karaoke singer. We quickly became friends and had a great laugh. Karen was always telling Jimmy off for drinking and smoking too much, while she was pouring him a drink and lighting his cigarette. What a great couple! It was Jimmy who got me up on the microphone. I had never sung karaoke in my life and Karen used to say, 'I'm sick of listening to his songs, you have a go Dave.' So up I got and murdered a few songs just to keep Karen happy. Then something strange happened one day. Jimmy started coaching me, in terms of which songs to sing and which ones to avoid. He would pick the artists to suit my voice and we would have a few beers and practise before the pub got busy. Now I'm not bragging, and I certainly wouldn't win The X Factor or anything, but I can sing a bit – albeit karaoke, and this would give me something to do when I was out drinking in Benidorm with Jimmy and Karen on our day off. I used to go around their apartment because they had a pool and we would tell jokes and they would try and teach me Spanish. Jimmy was a sign-writer by trade and he would get jobs during the day doing signage for pubs, clubs and people with vans. Nothing fancy, but he was talented at what he did. They also took me to places that weren't touristy – nice restaurants off the beaten track. 'Where you can bring a girl if you meet someone, Dave,' Karen would say. I told her I wasn't in Benidorm to meet anyone, I was here to chill...

We were at work one night, nothing unusual about that, when in walked a gorgeous woman with two elderly ladies, which I found out later to be her aunty Marion and her mum Joyce. Yvonne was her name and they ordered drinks and sat down. A little while later, Yvonne came to the bar and asked me if we had a cigarette machine. I told her we didn't, but if she went left out of the bar, left at the end of the street and left again she would find one. It wasn't like a bolt of lightning or anything, but there was something about this woman that made me feel that I needed to get to know her. What a beautiful woman, and her tits aren't bad either, I thought! We still laugh today about our first meeting. Yvonne just says, 'Remember our first meeting? Left, left, left and left again!'

Later that night, after watching her every move, I noticed that this old Dutch guy was pestering her. No, it wasn't Jimmy; he was busy on the stage doing his karaoke. She came to the bar and asked if I could rescue her. I can't remember what I said but it did the trick and I asked Yvonne if she wanted to meet me when I finished work. I told her to meet me at Café B as it was affectionately known. I gave her directions from the bar. 'Down to what they call the square, turn right and walk up to the corner, turn right again and go past the funfair, and it's on your left, got it?' 'Yes, no problem,' she said. So I finished work, closed up shop and headed for Café B. Not thinking she would be there, the reason I chose Café B was because it would definitely be open, and if she wasn't there it was on my way home!

To my delight, there she was with Aunty Marion and her mum as her chaperones. They were game for a laugh earlier and I was quite shocked that they made a sharp exit when I arrived. Off to bed, I thought. It was 2 am. Then Yvonne told me the funniest thing I had heard all day... They had come out of the Black Chicken and to make sure they found Café B they had jumped in a taxi. Zoom... the taxi drove them all of the 500 metres in a straight line and stopped and the driver said, 'Gracias, 500 pesetas por favor.' They were mortified when they realised how close it was. Obviously my directions leave a lot to be desired. Anyway, we had a laugh about that and got on like a house on fire. I took her home to her apartment and dropped her off, like the gentleman I am. They were only there for a week and I would meet Yvonne every day, and she would pop in with her chaperones every night for a few drinks, and we would meet after I finished work and have fun, like we were on holiday together. It was the best time and I took Yvonne to the restaurants and places that weren't touristy that Jimmy and Karen had taken me to. It was then time for Yvonne, Aunty Marion and her mum to fly home and we agreed to keep in touch.

We wrote to each other regularly and spoke on the phone. I was still working at the Black Chicken and it got really busy over the summer months. At the end of August things were dying down a bit and it was going through my mind that I should get back to England and rejoin the "real world". I would hopefully see Yvonne again and think about getting a proper job. I still didn't have a clue what I was going to do, but knew it was time to get back before I became an alcoholic!

Chapter 2

Back to "Blighty"

It was September 2000 and the new football season was about to start. I was offered a lift to the airport by a couple from Manchester who had been to Benidorm on holiday with their kids. I had met the husband a few times as he used to fly out quite regularly doing "the baccy run" (buying as many cigarettes as he could fit in his suitcases and taking them back to England to sell for profit). They were a nice family and while we were travelling back we got chatting and they asked me what I was going to do when I got back. 'I don't have a clue,' I said. So, as we were flying in to Manchester, they invited me to stay with them, and go to the match, as Manchester United were playing my team, Newcastle United, on the opening day of the premiership.

We drew 1-1. I thanked them for their hospitality and was on my way back to Newcastle to see my mum. I had a few quid in my pocket but as I didn't know where my next wage was going to come from, I decided that I wasn't going to buy a ticket. I caught the train, which was delayed en route by some mechanical failure. Every time the guard came looking for tickets, I would go and hide in the toilet until I thought it was safe to come out. The train then got diverted and I had to make two connections, dodging the conductors as I went. I managed to get all the way home for free. What a result. But it was the most stressful thing I had done all year!

I rang Yvonne when I got home and she invited me to

her house for a few days. I met her family and we went out for drinks. It was just as good as I remembered it in Benidorm, I thought. I think her family thought I had come to sponge off her. Some daft lad she met on holiday, they must have thought! 'Anyway, it won't last, so just enjoy yourself and he will be off back to Newcastle,' they told her. Little did they know...

As I only had an HGV licence and my sales background, it was going to be a struggle finding work, I thought. So I started thinking about what I could actually do to make money. I wasn't going to sign on and claim benefits, because that just isn't me. I started looking in the papers and did a bit of research into franchising. A turnkey business would be good as they would give me training and a ready-made business in return for my life savings! Not a bad idea, but I only had £10,000 in the bank and the franchise I had identified was going to cost me £17,500. It was a carpet and upholstery cleaning business which looked like I could make a decent living from. Where there's muck there's brass, I thought. So I spoke to the franchisor and they advised me that because it was a well-established franchise the banks would look favourably on it for a business loan. So off I trotted to the bank and sure enough they listened to what I had to say, looked at the business plan and agreed to loan me the difference plus a bit more so I could start some marketing etc. I was now in business.

I had to go to a place near Oxford to do my initial training and I spoke with Yvonne and let her know what I was doing. She was happy with the fact that I had got myself sorted so quickly, I think. Now she was going out with a businessman and not a daft barman from Benidorm!

The training was quite intense as you not only learnt about how to run the business, but how to use chemicals that were used to get rid of all types of nasty stains like red wine and glue. It was fascinating, and at the end of the two-week course you picked up all of your materials and machines and your van that would be your livelihood for the next few years.

Off I went to Newcastle with all the enthusiasm and knowledge I had been given, dreaming of how I was going to make my fortune.

Yvonne and I used to take it in turns to come and see each other. She lived in a little village called North Skelton near Saltburn and Redcar. It was about a forty-five minute journey and it meant one of us travelling on the Friday night to visit the other. We would then get up at an ungodly hour on the Monday morning to go to work. We used to travel back on the Sunday night, but as we grew closer, we both decided that the extra night together was worth the early start on the Monday morning.

We did this for about a year and three months and we had a great relationship. We got on well with one another's families and it was Christmas morning 2001 when I proposed to Yvonne with a diamond ring which was tied to a helium balloon. When she opened the box, the balloon floated out with the ring on the end of the string. She was so happy, because we had discussed it before, but I had kept it quiet and wanted it to be a surprise when I finally asked her. She accepted with delight and we made plans for our wedding. We had both been married before so we didn't want to do the church thing again, but nevertheless we wanted it to be special. We also had to decide where we were going to live when we were married, as Yvonne had a good job which she had been doing for fourteen years and I had this new business which was going well. We discussed it at great length and decided, due to the fact that my business was in Newcastle, it would be easier for her to come there. Yes it would be hard to move away from her family and friends, but it was only forty miles up the road.

I was still living at Mum's and Yvonne had a house that she had bought a few years earlier. We decided that it would be best for us both if we just rented initially, as it was going to be hard enough finding her a new job, never mind looking for a house to buy as well.

We found a place not too far from my mum's and decided to rent Yvonne's house out while we were in this transition period (our first buy-to-let!). Also, it was a big step for Yvonne as she had lived in that village her whole life! Even though she was sure it was the right decision, she had this very small doubt in the back of her mind that she might need to keep the house in case things didn't work out between us. I think that stemmed from some of her friends who kept asking her if she was sure she was doing the right thing.

My cleaning business was going great. I had put another van on the road and employed another guy to help with the workload. We were halfway through our six-month tenancy and the property market was really buoyant. I spoke with Yvonne about buying a house as I thought if we didn't do it now, we would never get one with the way house prices were climbing. We didn't have much savings as we had put a lot of money into my business and my mum had always said, 'If you ever need anything, don't hesitate to ask.' This was a big ask, and I decided it was the only way we were going to get on the housing ladder. I remember being dead nervous about asking her, but I knew it was the only way. I explained to her what I thought about the property prices going up and the fact that we didn't want to rent anymore because it was "dead money". Being a homeowner herself she understood that. My dad had passed away and left my mum on a solid footing. She was by no means rich, as we were just a normal working class family, but I knew with my dad passing, that she would be able to lend us the money, which she did without any hesitation. One of the many wonderful things my mum did for me while she was alive. So we now had a ten percent deposit and we knew what we could afford, so it was time to start looking.

Yvonne and I drove around various parts of Newcastle and surrounding areas and spotted a couple of properties we thought would be suitable. We wanted a three-bedroom house so her family could visit. We put an offer on a property that was being sold off by the military. It was an ex-MOD property and there were quite a few buyers in for it. It went to best and final offers and we offered the asking price. We were told that someone had offered higher and we lost it! Undeterred, we kept on looking. Then, a few days later I was cleaning a lady's carpets at the top of the street (where we now live). When I packed up and drove down the street, I saw a van parked up and the guy erecting a "for sale" board. I quickly wrote the number down as he was pulling away. I decided I would be cheeky and knock on the door. The owner answered and I asked if I could have a look around while I was there. I explained that we had been looking for a property and had been gazumped on the previous property we were trying to purchase. It was just what we were looking for and he explained that we would have to go through the estate agent if we were interested in putting an offer forward. I rang Yvonne all excited and told her about the house. The owner had given me his number and I arranged a second viewing so Yvonne could have a look at it.

She loved it; it was exactly what we were looking for. After a bit of decorating and some new carpets, it would be a little palace, she said. We told the owners that we were definitely interested, and that we would be offering them the full asking price through the agent (£95,000). Yvonne thought that was a fortune at the time, as she had only paid £44,000 for her three bed semi about four years previously!

I told the owner our mortgage was already agreed in principle and that we wouldn't mess him about. We wanted a fairly quick completion because our tenancy was nearly up. I said, 'We won't mess you about, as long as you don't try and increase the price. We have been gazumped before and we really want this house.' We shook hands on the deal and we completed about four weeks later. October 2003. When I went to pick the keys up, the owner told me that the estate agent who was dealing with the sale had rung him a week after he had accepted our offer, to say that he thought he could get him more money, because he had other buyers interested. But true to his word and a handshake in his house, he told them that he was happy with the asking price offer he had accepted from us and that was that (bloody estate agents!).

We were really excited and the house "that didn't need anything doing to it" had all the walls skimmed with plaster as Yvonne hated the artex walls. She then decided that if we were going to plaster all the walls we may as well knock the wall down between the toilet and the bathroom to make the bathroom twice as big, and if we were going to do that, we may as well have the bathroom completely made over to save making a mess later on! Obviously I agreed – as you do! We still had a few weeks to go on our current tenancy agreement, so it was all systems go to get it all done before we could move in. What a bloody mess the house was in. The walls were down, the bathroom was completely ripped out and reshuffled so we could have a separate shower cubicle and a corner bath. There was a skip outside and all the neighbours must have been thinking, what the hell are they doing to that house? This would be the theme over the next few years, because like Yvonne said, "It didn't need anything doing to it". We had started our first refurbishment!

Another year or so went by and I was getting

disillusioned with my cleaning franchise. Don't get me wrong, we were doing okay, we had another van and employee on the road and turnover of about £100,000 a year. But as Yvonne was the accountant of the family she had worked out that we were doing all this work to earn less than our employees. So we had some serious decisions to make.

Yvonne had no trouble finding a job when she moved to Newcastle. In fact it was so refreshing for her coming from a small village to a big city; she had her eyes opened with what offers she got from prospective employers. She eventually decided on a job working for a property company as head of accounts and general manager on a really good salary. She was offered a company car. The little Vauxhall Astra we owned was about on its last legs, so we decided she should take the car. This company bought and sold houses for investors. They refurbished them and put tenants in them.

At first it was hard, as she had a bully of a boss, but as she gained more trust within the firm she had more responsibility and more respect, so things settled down. She used to come home and tell stories of all the money that the salesmen would earn and the flash cars they would drive. The first company Christmas party we were invited to really opened our eyes. Yvonne was called into the office by her boss who calmly handed her a really expensive briefcase with £10,000 in it! He said, 'Take that home with you and bring it to the party tonight, you will be okay, and your husband will be with you! It's a prize for one of the salesmen!' When she brought it home, I jokingly said, 'Just give me a black eye and we'll phone the police and tell them we've been mugged!' Yvonne calmly said, 'Don't even think about it, they are like the mafia, it's not worth it.' 'Only joking dear, only joking!' I said.

We arrived at the party which was being held at a castle

in Northumberland. As Yvonne was management we had a room booked and paid for by the firm – a very lavish affair with an awards atmosphere and everyone dolled up to the nines. There were a lot of people at this party and there was a lot of handshaking and kisses all round. It seemed that money was no object to these people and later in the evening I really had my eyes opened. Now I'm not one to be easily impressed, but the owners of the firm had really gone mad, I thought when the presentations started. There was a raffle as well and some really nice prizes – watches, televisions, pamper weekends for the ladies and all manner of electrical gadgets and weekends away that you would expect in a raffle. But the main event was the presentations for the salesmen and dare I say women. No, don't mention women at this bash, as it was a very male-oriented company with a male chauvinist at the helm. So no, there were no saleswomen! The owners obviously placed great store in the sales force and being from a sales background myself I could understand that. Without sales you don't have a business, especially in their type of business – property.

The time had arrived for the presentation of the top three salesmen. First prize I was thinking would be that briefcase Yvonne and I had delivered earlier with the ten grand inside. How wrong I was! The briefcase was actually third prize! Second prize was a speedboat, and the top salesman was given a villa in Spain! Unbelievable, I thought, and it was probably at that moment that I decided I had to get into property somehow. My wife was in the perfect place to put in a good word for me, as I am a great believer in "it's not what you know, it's who you know". Yes, I decided, property was for me. If these guys had built a business that could afford to give away these fantastic prizes then it was definitely for me!

I asked Yvonne to introduce me to the main men,

including the sales manager, which she did, and I made a point of giving them a potted history of my own sales background. Not the time or place really, but I didn't go overboard and thought they were quite nice guys really. I thought, you have to seize the day, and just came right out and asked if they had any jobs going in the sales department. I told them I was in the process of selling my successful carpet and upholstery cleaning franchise – which was a little white lie, I thought. I will be if they offer me a job! The sales manager told me to give him a call and he would set up an interview! I was cock-a-hoop and thoroughly enjoyed the rest of the party with Yvonne. I couldn't help but start thinking about how it would change our lives, and on the way to the car the next morning we bumped into the top salesman who was just getting into his top of the range sports car! That was it. I would be ringing the sales manager first thing on Monday morning!

The interview was set up for Thursday the following week and I could hardly wait. I don't think I have ever been as nervous or as excited at the same time. I was gutted it was going to take so long to get an interview, but that was just impatience on my part. My days were still busy with my current business, but I was willing the time to pass and couldn't wait for the interview.

It was the previous Friday when Yvonne came home and told me this story which I have to share with you, so you can get an understanding of why I was so determined to get a job in property.

Yvonne was called into the boss's office and was handed a crisp box with some newspaper covering whatever was inside it. She took the newspaper from the top to reveal that it was a box full of cash! She was told to count it and put it in envelopes of £1,000 each. She started counting it and there was £100,000 in the box in total. She gave it back to one of the directors who put it in the boot of his car, presumably to take it to the bank.

The next day he came in and told Yvonne about the events of the previous evening. He said that he had gone to do some food shopping with his wife and son, When they got back to their house he had asked the son to unload the groceries and "the crisp box". The next morning he had asked the son where the crisp box was. To his horror, the son replied, "Oh, I think I left it on the doorstep outside!" He had gone running to the door and the box was still there! When Yvonne told me that story, I knew there was money to be made in property. What other business (apart from crime, I thought) could make that sort of cash?

The day finally arrived and I put on my best suit and lucky tie. I walked passed three sports cars, and various other expensive-looking cars on my way to the reception. I waited in reception, looking about and taking it all in. There were three or four company names on the wall, and I hadn't realised until then how big this operation was! Everyone was smartly dressed and the whole operation looked slick. I was nervous and excited at the prospect of getting involved with what looked a very successful outfit.

The sales manager showed me around the building and introduced me to members of the sales team, some of whom I had already met at the Christmas party a couple of weeks ago. We walked into his office and I was very relaxed. It was more of a polite conversation than an interview. He asked me about relevant experience and then calmly asked when I would like to start! I was gobsmacked but over the moon. I told him I could start the following week. I was aware I would have to sort the franchise out and wind that business up, but I was so excited that they had offered me what I thought would be the chance of a lifetime. This is my time to get rich, I thought. But how wrong I was.

Yvonne phoned me on the Friday, the day after my successful interview. She was upset and I could tell that she was crying. I asked her what was up and she told me that the firm had gone bust! What!? I couldn't believe my ears. The exhilaration of landing my dream job twenty-four hours earlier, and now the prospect of my wife losing her job, and back to cleaning carpets and upholstery for me? Gutted wasn't the word!

It turned out that the Office of Fair Trading and the DTI had closed them down for misappropriation of funds. They'd had loads of complaints from investors and the fraud squad got involved and had been keeping a close eye on the operation for months. As Yvonne's role in the company had involved her dealing with the directors and handling the book-keeping, the DTI employed her to help them with the winding up of the companies – which for us wasn't a bad thing because they had to employ her on the same terms of employment and salary. So she was guaranteed another six months' work and could start applying for other jobs. In our opinion, the girl that Yvonne had taken over from was planted in the firm by the fraud squad. She did a handover with Yvonne and disappeared down south somewhere. That's why we thought they (DTI) had asked Yvonne to stay on, because they knew that she was nothing to do with what the directors were up to, merely a pawn in a very tangled web of deceit. Thinking about it now, it was funny that Yvonne and all the admin staff were in a separate building from the sales team and the investment team. Probably to make sure they didn't hear or see anything they shouldn't!

Chapter 3

Déjà Vu?

After Yvonne had finished the work she was doing with the DTI, she got a job with a charitable organisation that did extra-curricular activity with children. Meanwhile, I was still working away at the franchise, looking for another opportunity to get into property. We decided to get married that year – 2003. We invited some of the staff and directors from Yvonne's previous job who had kept in touch with her since the collapse of the company.

We were keeping our heads above water and paying the bills. Then one day, about nine months later and out of the blue, I received a phone call from an ex-director of the property company that Yvonne used to work for. He asked to meet me for a coffee as he had a proposition for me. My ears perked up and I agreed to meet him. He started off by telling me that they had closed the other company down because they were so far behind with the refurbishment of the properties they were sourcing for investors, that it became apparent that they were in breach of the terms under which they had taken clients' money. It was deemed as misappropriation of funds in some cases because they had sold properties to investors who were unhappy with the situation. Some investors had invested quite a lot of money and quite rightly were looking for a return on their investment which wasn't forthcoming due to the aforementioned. He explained that the business model of the previous company was sound and could be replicated again but on a smaller scale. He went on to tell me that he was fighting his case with the DTI as they were wrong to shut his company down as they were still actively purchasing property. If they had just told them to suspend trading, then his company would have been able to "catch up with all the refurbishments and get back on track".

I listened intently to what he was telling me, wondering where this conversation was going. Because most of the staff from the previous company had distanced themselves from him and Yvonne and I had kept in touch, and invited him to our wedding a few months previously, he had thought of me going for the interview on the day they had closed and knew I was keen to get into property.

With that, he asked me if I would be interested in helping set up a brand new company using the same business model as his previous company. He was setting it up with another associate of his who was nothing to do with the previous company. They would be doing it on a much smaller scale, but were confident that it would still be lucrative as the buy-to-let market was still buoyant. Prices were still rising and it would be more profitable doing it on a smaller scale with fewer overheads. He said he couldn't afford to pay me initially because he needed the money he had to buy the first few properties with. I still had my cleaning business and Yvonne was settling in to her new job. So financially, although it might be a struggle juggling both jobs for me, I thought it was a second opportunity at getting into property and too good to miss. I spoke with Yvonne and she agreed that we should give it a go as it was my dream job and if it didn't work out, we still had the business and her job to fall back on. So it was really a calculated risk which may or may not pay off.

It was 2004. The office was at the back of a house in a quiet but select area of Newcastle. It was only fifteen minutes from home, although I wouldn't be spending much time there because I was going to be out on the road looking for property. I was working with another lad who was the director's son. We went out on the road a few times and he showed me what to look for in the way of defects on property – damp, electrics, windows etc. He gave me a brief overview of how to estimate what it would cost to refurbish and bring the properties up to a rental standard. He then showed me what margins we would need to work to so that we could sell them at market value or just below, to make a profit. It wasn't rocket science, I thought: market value of property – refurbishment costs – margin = price that we need to get the property for. Offer lower than this to the selling agent or vendor and we have a deal.

That sounded nice and easy, except by the time you worked out what it would cost to do all the work and add our margin, it meant in some cases we were offering about 30-40% lower than the market value. So persuading people to take offers substantially below what their properties were worth wasn't going to be easy at all. I knew now that I was going to be working a lot harder than I thought. My perception of getting into property was probably the same as other people's – easy money… which it isn't!

There's a definite art to negotiating a deal with an estate agent, vendor or anyone else selling their property. There are all sorts of reasons why people sell houses. Bereavement, divorce, inheritance, getting repossessed, financial difficulties... the list goes on. So the art of negotiating a purchase had a lot to do with getting the properties where the sellers were motivated. All the aforementioned reasons being a starting point. At first I was just making appointment after appointment, until I realised that if the seller wasn't motivated you were wasting your time. So I started doing research on my target properties and narrowing down the number of viewings I was doing based on whether or not they were motivated sellers. The bad news was that by the time I had done my research and rang to make an appointment, the property was already under offer from another company or buyer doing the same as me! It was time for a rethink. I followed my old sales philosophy of "if you throw enough mud at the wall, some of it will stick". I also had to get re-organised and keep track of every offer that I had put in over the previous weeks because a "No" now doesn't mean a "No" forever. Unmotivated sellers soon became motivated sellers over a period of time. By keeping track of all the offers I was putting in, I was actually getting somewhere. People were phoning me back two and three weeks later, sometimes longer, and asking if I was still in the market for their property. Considering I was a novice at this, I was delighted when the deals were being struck. Meanwhile, the other colleagues in this new venture were supposed to be selling them to investors so we could actually get the deals completed and make our margin – and get paid. Because until you have an end user for any product, and property is no different, the profit you know is in the deal isn't realised until the sale has completed with the purchaser.

Because I was getting pretty good at closing deals and we had quite a few to sell, I came off the road and back into the office. I switched from buyer to seller, pitching the properties to potential investors. They were from all over the country and some local investors. We would invite them up to the north-east via car, train or plane – whichever they preferred, depending on where they were coming from. We would meet them at the train station or airport and take them on a tour of the north-east, show them a selection of properties and close them on the deals. We asked them for a reservation fee as a commitment to purchase which was non-refundable. This would help with our cashflow in the short term as we were spending money on petrol driving all over the place for viewings and again showing the investor clients around. Bearing in mind we were three months in and I still wasn't earning a wage! Talk about a baptism of fire! But I could see it all taking shape and at least I was getting my petrol money out of the business. Not ideal, but no-one can ever accuse me of not working hard for my money, I thought.

Yvonne and I were now at the point however that we could see money coming into the company and had decided between us that it was nearly time to give up on the dream, because I still wasn't being paid. I decided to approach the subject with the main man and let him know that I thought I had proven myself worthy of a wage now, and if it wasn't forthcoming I would be sacking it and going back to my cleaning (which I didn't want to do). To my surprise he agreed that with all the pipeline deals on the go and the deals I had actually closed with investors, it was time to agree a salary. He also recognised that we really needed some help. We were running around like headless chickens and it was a very fine balancing act going out and buying and then trying to sell as well. So he was going to bring another salesman on board. Great idea, I thought, because I was actually enjoying the buying more than the selling. Being out on the road, viewing houses and haggling with the sellers. It was more of a buzz closing those deals than taking a deposit from an investor.

So I went back out on the road, and things were still going well three months on. Yvonne and I had decided to sell the franchise and I was asked to keep my eyes open on my travels for suitable office space as we needed somewhere bigger to operate from. At the same time as we were starting to really motor in terms of closing deals with investors completing on their investment, the main man asked me if I thought Yvonne would consider coming back to work with us. That was a shocker, and totally out of the blue. He had always asked after her and what she was up to. She was on a really good salary in her new job and I told him that I didn't think she would because she seemed quite happy with what she was doing, but that I would definitely ask her. We arranged to meet him at a restaurant so we could hear what he had to offer her. He told her that she was invaluable to him in his previous company and that the way things were going he needed someone who was organised and knew a bit about the property game. He said she was the first name on his list. Yvonne and I had discussed how we thought the meeting would go prior to going to the restaurant. We had agreed that it was nice of him to think about her, but he wouldn't be able to match her current salary. I had already been working for free for three months and she wasn't about to leave a salaried position to go and work for him for free. We were both in shock when he turned around at the end of the meal and said that after listening to everything he had said, if she thought she would like to work with him again, he would match her current salary! To my surprise and as cool as a cucumber she calmly told him that she would think about it. We said our goodbyes and went home to discuss what had just happened. After a long discussion about "all of our eggs in one basket", we came to a mutual decision that she would only come on board if they kept it a small- to medium-sized company, which would be run ethically and not get into the same problems as the previous company did because they got too big. She gave a month's notice to her current employer, who was devastated by her news, but wished her well in her new venture. For the first time in our relationship, we would be working together. The journey had truly begun.

Chapter 4

Once Bitten, Twice Shy

I had sourced a building on a business park and we were ready to move. We were ending the first year of trading and business was booming. We were selling everything we were sourcing and Yvonne was well and truly back in the saddle. She was in the process of recruiting new staff to help with the administration and day-to-day running of the business. I was asked to recruit a couple more buyers and the salesman that was brought in to help me was asked to recruit a couple more salespeople. By the time we had settled in to the new office, we were selling an average of ten properties a week to investors and completing on as many at the same time. So commission-wise, the company was already turning over about £100,000 a week. Because the completions were weekly and the main man was old-fashioned, he liked to pay us weekly. Yvonne's salary had gone up and my commission was now increasing by the week as we were on a roll. I don't like to brag as it's not in my nature, but the take-home pay Yvonne and I were bringing home was five figures a week. After struggling in the beginning while I was earning no salary at all, we felt like millionaires in comparison. The hours were longer and the days were tiring, but the rewards were everything I had dreamt of and the reason I wanted to get into property. I was now living the dream!

As the months rolled on I was learning more and more about the property game. How to do back-to-back deals, sell and rent back deals and no money down deals. It was like a real-life university course. Not only was I educating myself in the property game, I was learning different investment strategies, because all investors have their own ideas about what they want to do long term and how property can be a vehicle to make you comfortably well off when you retire. I was like a sponge, and enjoying every minute of it. There weren't enough hours in the day, which I know is an old cliché but it really was true.

And so it went on for another year and I was now in charge of a team of about twenty buyers and there were about ten salesmen, not to mention the admin team who were the liaison between sales, buyers, solicitors and the directors. Yvonne pulled it all together and made sure that everything ran like clockwork. Let's not forget that she used to run a factory of 250 men. As this was the first time we had actually worked together, I could now see why the main man regarded her so highly and I was proud of how good she was at her job. Multitasking is her forte and I can honestly say that her organisational and HR skills were second to none. If she had gone down a different path in her life she could have been head of any corporation you care to mention. I am not just saying this as her husband, but as a co-worker and admirer of her abilities. She will actually be embarrassed when she reads this because she is also very modest.

As we grew the business with the help of an army of staff, so it seemed, I was asked to go further afield to source properties and buyers in those areas because the buying team couldn't keep up with the sales team, which had now grown into this hungry beast that devoured everything we could throw at it. This was a bit of a strain on Yvonne and me because it meant I had to stay in hotels a few nights a week and we weren't used to being apart.

Investors were going mad for property and the buy-to-let boom was in full swing. Property prices were still rising and we couldn't keep up with demand. The whole thing was going crazy and the money going through the company was unbelievable. But at the same time, I was starting to see the cracks in the company and so was Yvonne. We found ourselves questioning the ethos of the company, and exactly what Yvonne had asked not to happen was now happening. The company was growing into the same beast as the one that was shut down. When we questioned things, our concerns were dismissed as if we were out of order for asking them. If I made a mistake, it was like World War Three had erupted and all of a sudden my dream job wasn't so dreamy. But when you are on that sort of money you put it to the back of your mind and get on with it.

We carried on for the next few months but we were increasingly concerned with the way things were being run. An example of this was the sales team who were now resorting to what amounted to blatant lies. They would invite investors up to the north-east in the same way that they always did. When they showed them around houses they would close the deals on the basis of what properties the investors had looked at. They were now taking a £3,000 deposit to secure the deal. But what the investors thought they had paid a deposit for didn't exist! Because we were sourcing properties at a slower pace than the salesmen were selling them, the investor would then be contacted and told that the property they had viewed had fallen through because the vendor had pulled out of the deal for whatever reason – but rest assured they would be allocated another property.

At the same time as all this was going on, I was offered a directorship with the company. Why now? I thought. The offer was unbelievable in terms of income and I was tempted to take them up on their offer. But after discussing it with Yvonne at great length and my accountant we decided that because the way things were being run it felt like it was offered to keep us quiet.

We let them know a few days later that I wasn't going to accept the offer of a directorship and it was like I had just started a rival company. The main man went absolutely berserk and called me all sorts of nasty things. Right decision, I thought. This was late in 2006 and I told Yvonne that I would be leaving after Christmas. I couldn't put up with it any longer. Yvonne said she would be giving her notice in as well as the company had turned into exactly what she was promised it wouldn't. We left in January 2007 and were now unemployed! It was quite a scary place to be, considering we were on a six-figure salary between us.

Chapter 5

"No Money Down" and "Sell and Rent Back"

Because we now knew the property game inside out, we decided that we could do exactly what we had been doing, but this time for ourselves. We started by working from home and quickly got on with sourcing and refurbishing properties. All the while we were keeping our eyes open for premises to operate from.

In the days of sell and rent back (circa 2005-2006 when mortgage lenders still allowed it), schemes were popping up in advertisements all over the press – along with "no money down" advertisements to investors. Investment clubs and property brokers were making a fortune doing these types of deals for their clients/members. We looked into it and thought that was how we could purchase our properties, but we didn't need to join an investment club as they charge fortunes in fees for property we could source ourselves. This is a brief explanation of what these terms mean and how it works:

Someone who wants to release the equity in their property for a number of reasons is the type of person who would consider a sell and rent back deal. Divorce, splitting up, redundancy, bereavement or illness are all reasons why someone might want to sell a property. How might that be any different to just selling through an estate agent? Well, if someone found themselves in any of those situations the financial burdens may be overwhelming. Coupled with the fact that some of those situations could mean that their finances might be coming under strain and the stress of dealing with their own grief (or whatever situation they found themselves in), this might lead to them requiring a quick sale. Most of the respondents to advertisements placed in the press wanted to stay in the place they called home. They just couldn't afford to live on their current income or didn't want the burden of a mortgage any more. Especially as nearly all of those people who applied for this type of deal had quite a nice amount of equity in their properties. So sell and rent back was an ideal vehicle for them. I can hear you asking, 'What's the catch?'

The catch, if you can call it that, was that they would have to give up some of that equity so investors could facilitate the deal.

Let's say that the property was worth £100,000 and they owed £50,000 on their mortgage, £3,000 on credit cards and £7,000 on a secured loan that would need to be paid off. A total of £60,000 debt. All of these debts, coupled with any of the above situations, would be enough to make someone pick up the phone. They were motivated sellers!

Their payments might look something like this:

Mortgage £500
Credit cards minimum payment £100
Secured loan £300
Total = £900

Investors would do their own calculations to see if the deal was viable for them to take on, because their debt and the deposit needed to come out of any equity that was left in the property.

A buy-to-let mortgage at that time could be obtained with a 15% deposit. The bigger the deposit, however, the safer the deal was, as it made the interest-only payments cheaper and the instant equity larger. In effect, investors were buying equity.

So the value of the property was £100,000 which meant that the investor could get an 85% mortgage on the property, i.e. £85,000, with the lender's fees added to the loan, normally about £1,000, and the interest-only payments would be about £430 at the time.

Investors would then look at what the going rate for rent was in the private rented sector in that specific area. Let's say it was £500 on this example. But you had to allow for interest rate rises and for each 1% increase that would mean an extra £70 per month on this mortgage. So a decision was then needed. Either take more out of the deal for the deposit or charge a higher rent than the going rate. A lot of investors tried to be fair with the applicants as it had to be a win-win for the investor and the client. If they didn't offer them enough out of the deal, they would just go and look for a better offer – human nature.

So, the investor agrees a price with the owner of £72,250 as the property is valued at £100,000.

The investor arranges a mortgage of £72,250 (85% loan) from mortgage lender A on a purchase price of £85,000 to buy the property (£12,750 deposit required).

At the same time, there is also an application in with mortgage lender B with a remortgage of £80,000 (80% loan) on a valuation of £100,000 (the market value of the property) to refinance and pay off the existing loan, the deposit of £20,000 and all related solicitor's fees.

The solicitor pays the seller's solicitor his £72,250 and his fees (approximately £1,000).

The solicitor then pays off the existing mortgage which will have had fees added to it of approximately £1,000 (£73,250) and charge the investor his fees and disbursements (approximately £1,000). Total £74,250.

The investor is left with any surplus monies (in this case, approximately £5,750) which are not subject to tax as he has remortgaged his property to release the funds.

All of this is carried out on the same day, hence the term "no money down".

This could be quite lucrative if enough of these deals were done as the deposits were coming from the client's property, not the investor! Remortgaging profit is not subject to capital gains tax as it is a further advance from a lender which you are paying back – unlike when you sell.

A Summary of Benefits to the Seller/Client:

£12,250 cash in the bank after mortgage and debts paid off. A rent of £550 per month which means they are £350 per month better off with all of their debts cleared. They remain in their home with no solicitor's fees or moving costs. They can continue with their life and no-one needs to know that they have even sold!

As the credit crunch took hold in 2007 and lenders started to really tighten up on their lending criteria in 2008, it became apparent that "no money down" deals were frowned upon and clients who wanted to do this type of deal would need to show that they had funds for deposits, which meant that "bridging finance" would then need to be used to purchase the properties. Then when you refinanced the properties the same day, you would pay back the bridging loan, settle the first mortgage and the end result was the same. You had a property which you had purchased with little or "no money down" and had instant equity in the property.

The global credit crunch was really starting to take hold and lenders and banks were frantically trying to sort their own internal finances out as well as pretty much stop lending. The mortgage market was in chaos.

There were many main lenders used for "no money down" deals and remortgages done with Mortgage Express (now owned by the government and the taxpayer). There weren't many who didn't charge penalties for taking out a loan and then settling it the same day. They made their money by charging arrangement fees at the outset and adding the fee to the loan amount, so when you settled the loan the same day they had their profit straight out. They made it easy for "no money down" companies and investors to do same-day refinancing. I can't remember the date, but it was about the same time as the other banks and lenders were pulling in the reins that Mortgage Express announced that they would no longer be offering their mortgage products to the market. This sent shockwaves through the investment community, a bit like a stock market crash. Total panic and frustration. If you had agreed to purchase properties from owners you then either had to find the deposits, find a bridging company to finance your deposit or pull out of the deal! Same-day refinancing was getting harder.

A few months later, lenders (not all at the same time, but quite closely following one another) decided that same-day refinancing was not going to be allowed. They changed the criteria once again to make it harder for these types of deals to be done. They announced that you would now have to own a property for a minimum of six months before you could apply for a further advance or to refinance it with another lender. This effectively killed the "no money down" market as most investors were purchasing properties in the same way as us. This is when we made the decision to stop purchasing property and let the mortgage market settle down and see what happened. As we now know, the rules have remained the same with most buy-to-let lenders asking for 25% deposits instead of 15%.

Sell and Rent Back – not all plain sailing...

One of our investors decided to purchase a property from

a lady who was in mortgage arrears. She had various debts which would all be paid off, leaving her debt-free and only the rent to pay. She wanted to stay in the property because her kids were attending the local school. It was a perfect sell and rent back scenario. The deal was done.

Everything was going according to plan. The rent was going into his account by standing order every month on the date agreed. But in month seven, he noticed that the rent hadn't gone into his bank account. He rang the tenant to ask what had happened. She informed him that she had been off sick and it would be paid in a couple of weeks. A couple of weeks passed and it still wasn't paid. He tried to phone her on numerous occasions and couldn't get hold of her. Finally, on the off-chance, he phoned, but the ringtone wasn't familiar. It was the sort of ringtone you get when someone is abroad, he thought. She answered the phone and nonchalantly informed him that she was on holiday in Spain and wouldn't be back until next week, when she would pay the rent into his bank. He hung up and thought, the cheeky cow is on holiday with my rent! He wrote a Section 21 notice out and hand-delivered it to the tenant's home (his property). He was so mad he decided to take a wheel clamp he had in his garage and clamped her car. He thought, she will have to ring me now when she gets back.

She arrived home on a Sunday and rang him to ask if he had clamped her car. 'Too right I have,' he said. 'And when you pay me the rent you owe me I will take it off.' She said she would phone the police so he told her to do just that. The police phoned and asked if he had a licence for the clamp. He said he might have, but if she wanted it off she would have to pay him some rent. The police officer told him if she damaged her own car he might be liable for the damage, to which he replied – 'The car is probably only worth what she owes me so we will be quits if she does!' The policeman hung up. About half an hour later, the tenant rang to say she could borrow the money from her mum if he would meet her at the property and remove the clamp. He told her he wanted a minimum of £500 and he would still be evicting her. She didn't care, she just wanted the clamp off so she could go to work. She met him at the property and duly gave him his £500. She had the cash when he arrived and he removed the clamp.

After a couple of months, he eventually got her out via the courts. This was one sell and rent back that didn't quite go according to plan. The upside is that he still has £20,000 equity so he is still up £18,000. The reason I know this sorry tale so well is because the investor was me!

Another case of a tenant who just couldn't play the game and pay her rent. When she eventually left, her parting comment was that all she wanted was a council house and this was the only way to get one! I could have saved us both a lot of stress and just told the council she was being repossessed at the beginning, if she had bothered to tell me from the start. You live and learn!

As of February 2012, sell and rent back was made illegal and the few remaining firms doing it legally were forced to shut down their operations by the DTI and the FSA.

Chapter 6

Property Finders North East

Things were going well and we had looked at a few shops and offices all over the north-east but none were suitable and most of them were very expensive in terms of the rent that people wanted and the rates were astronomical. We then spotted a shop on the internet that was up for sale with an estate agent. It was previously an estate agency premises so we went and had a look at it. It was perfect. It needed some refurbishing as it had no central heating or hot water, but that was all. It had a flat above and because it was in a regeneration area, the rateable value was very cheap. It seemed to take an age to get the finance sorted and over the course of the year the credit crunch was starting to take its toll on the economy. The market was slowing and investors were starting to get cold feet because of the way interest rates were rising. We had quite a few people pull out of deals but we were now committed to buying the shop.

We had to remortgage our own home to raise the capital to purchase the shop and all the equipment needed for the office – computers, telephone system, shop fittings etc.

We had it all refurbished (apart from the heating, because there was no gas into the building. It would be January before that would be sorted).We opened our doors on the 1st November 2007 and had councillor Jim Smith cut the ribbon. Jim sadly died a few years later after being in ill health for quite some time. RIP.

Because the market was slowing, we made a conscious

decision to look at other sources of income. We decided that we would open up as a full-blown estate agency. This would mean getting properties on the market which weren't necessarily investment properties. We also contacted all of our clients whom we had sold properties to and let them know that we would now be offering them lettings and property management. Because our previous company didn't offer this, we decided that we would also contact those clients as well. Yvonne had kept all of her contacts and telephone numbers. A bit naughty, but we were now in survival mode and had to do what needed doing to protect our own livelihood.

This gave us a great start in the business and we had to learn very quickly how to become estate agents.

The market was really slowing down but we still had a few active investors who were trying to build their portfolios. We sold a few houses on the open market as well. The lettings side of the business was really gathering momentum and by the end of the first year we had about one hundred properties on our books, which were covering our overheads.

I was out on the road doing appointments, sourcing property and doing everything that goes with property management. Yvonne was having to run the office most of the time on her own and in between dealing with customer enquiries on the phone she had to do all the processing of landlords' monthly rental statements and transfer their rental payments into their accounts. So we really had our work cut out. It was time to get some help and we decided that we would get an apprentice on board to help us with the administration in the office and to deal with telephone enquiries so Yvonne could concentrate on dealing with the property management and payments to landlords. Later that same year, we also hired another member of staff to help me with viewings, checking tenants into properties and interim inspections. Business was really going great and we were getting our fair share of new landlords. We were now so busy that we were contemplating switching the business to just property management and not doing sales anymore. We made a conscious decision that it would make sense for us to do it very soon.

In November 2011, we were offered the opportunity to take over eighty properties to manage from a colleague who was in the same line of work. For one reason and another he wanted to concentrate on selling as he had been let down with staffing issues and mismanagement of his business. We agreed a price with him and started the long process of writing to all the landlords and tenants to let them know what was happening. Most landlords were relieved that we were taking over but a few didn't want to transfer to someone they didn't know, which was their prerogative. After visiting two properties owned by a landlord who had agreed for us to take over his whole portfolio, we found out that they were being repossessed and in the process of being handed over to an asset management company. So we lost ten properties due to that. To be honest it wasn't a total loss as the properties in question were in one of the roughest places in the north-east.

A month later I had a meeting with a representative of a company who had just bought a building for about one million pounds. It was going to be transformed into self-contained accommodation. There were forty self-contained studio flats, one-bedroom flats and two-bedroom flats. So it was definitely time to stop doing sales as this meant we now had over 300 properties on our books to let and manage. We decided that in the new year (January 2012) that we would write to all of our vendors who had property for sale with us and inform them of our decision to stop doing sales.

Chapter 7

Profile of a Tenant

Your best friend before they move in… your worst enemy when you want them out!!

Now I don't want to say that all tenants are the same, as a lot of tenants are honest, hard-working people who just need somewhere they can call home. They might be renting for a number of reasons or simply just don't want to be homeowners. So this profile is not about those people who pay their rent, look after their rented property, and live quietly and in harmony with their neighbours. No, this profile is the profile of those tenants who end up on "Landlords Best Friend" a free website we set up for the tenants who match the profile I am about to describe to you now. The ones you definitely want to avoid if you can help it, and the ones that you won't know fit this profile until they are in your property… and it's too late!

When you purchase a property for buy-to-let you have a few choices about where and what you buy, but a lot of investors and landlords buy in the wrong areas because they either haven't done their due diligence or they have been misled by some investment club or some so-called "property club" who told them everything they wanted to hear about the area and the property they were trying to sell them. This is when you are more likely to meet our friends "the tenants from hell".

Gender doesn't come into this profile. Both sexes are as bad as one another. In most cases they attract the same sort of partners. They will generally smoke and have: kids, dogs and/or other pets, a large flat screen TV, laptops for all the family and designer clothes. They will definitely like to drink and have all-night parties. How can they afford all this when they are on benefits? Because some bright spark in the government decided that we should pay the tenant the rent instead of the landlord. Their (the government's) argument is that it will help tenants be more socially responsible, and the housing benefit should go to them because it's *their* benefit claim. My argument is, if the housing benefit is supposed to go towards paying rent, then that's what it should be used for. If tenants spend it on anything else, it's fraud! Anyway, tenants wouldn't get the housing benefit if the landlord didn't provide a house (address) for them to claim for.

At the time of writing this, private landlords are currently owed about £40 million in unpaid rent, so the following may or may not have happened to you...

When the tenants initially make an enquiry, they will be as nice as your closest friend. They will be keen to be in your property because they have already been served notice on the property they are in. They have already trashed that one and spent all the housing benefit and it's time to move on. They will normally have a very convincing story about the previous landlord or letting agent not carrying out repairs and the property being so damp that it's affecting their children's health. So they will tell you when you phone for a reference that the agent or landlord will tell you a load of lies about them because they have been a good tenant and they don't want to lose them. "But honestly, we only stopped paying the rent because they wouldn't do the repairs or cure the damp problem!" What a load of rubbish!

They might also tell you that they are living with their

parents because they have been on the council waiting list for years. But they are sick of being at home and it is time to get a place of their own. Why do they use this one? Well why do you think? If they tell you they are living with their parents, the previous landlord or letting agent doesn't come into the conversation! You won't even know that they have rented a property, trashed it, played loud music every night because they are unemployed, and sickened all the neighbours who can't get to sleep every night for the noise.

So you listen to their stories and because your property has been empty for two months you are desperate to get a tenant, any tenant, to live in your property and prevent you having to suffer another void (empty property with no income) month. You meet them at your property and as soon as their first foot hits the inside of the property they are telling you that it is perfect and just what they are looking for! Just what they are looking for alright... another mug landlord who is going to regret this decision for the rest of his investment life! They are on housing benefits, and they would love for the payments to come directly to you because they don't want to touch the money. They smile and make a few jokes with you and tell you what a great place you have. In fact, they have never seen such a nice place. They ask you if you are thinking of selling anytime soon because they want a long-term tenancy and would like to live in your house for years... Sound familiar? The perfect tenant for you!

Moving day arrives and they move all their belongings into your house. They ring you to tell you that they have filled in all the benefit forms and told the council that they want the payments to come to you. You are so happy because you have this tenant, you can't believe your luck and when the rent is backdated you will get a nice big cheque from the council to pay into your bank and cover the mortgage payments that you have covered while waiting for the claim to be processed.

Six weeks pass and you phone the council to see what is taking so long to get this claim into payment. What claim? they ask you. Shock, horror, the tenant has lied to you. You phone the tenant to ask what is going on. The number you were ringing before they moved in which was answered every time you rang it, now never gets answered. You ring them again and again and get angry and frustrated. You decide to text them and ask them to ring you. They don't ring because this type of tenant doesn't want to talk to you anymore. You are now going to have your work cut out getting hold of these tenants and getting them to sort the claim for housing benefit out. The clock is ticking and you are now at week eight. The tenant finally texts you back and tells you that either they, their mother, granny or dad is in hospital so they can't ring you. They will ring you tomorrow. Tomorrow comes and goes and eventually after numerous calls and texts you get hold of them. You explain what the council have told you and that they need to get down there and fill the forms in. They will tell you they have already done it but will go down again and sort it out. While they are on the phone, they will tell you that the boiler isn't working properly or there is a draught in the children's bedroom and some damp. Could you sort it out? This is them telling you that they are not going to be the perfect tenants you thought you were getting. They have stalled you for two months and that's about £800. They will now go down to the benefit office and put the claim in, but what they won't tell the council is that they want the rent to come to you. By the time the claim gets sorted, in about another four weeks, the rent owed will be about £1,200.

They will tell you that the forms are now in and that they have a receipt to prove it if you want a copy. You decline the offer as long as it's sorted, you think. Four weeks pass and you ring the council to chase up their claim. Oh yes it's sorted, they tell you. You ask when *you* can expect payment. They tell you that payment has already been sent. They rushed the claim through because the tenant said that you were going to evict them if they didn't get the rent in a few weeks. So they sent them the money ten days ago. £1,150. Your heart sinks. You ring the tenant to ask when they are going to pay you? There's no answer for a few days and when you finally get a text off them they tell you that they are in hospital. This is month four and you decide that if they don't pay you, you are going to serve notice on them. You ring the council to advise them that the tenants have spent the rent and not given it to you. So the council inform you that they are very sorry and all future payments will come to you. The next payment is due in four weeks' time. This is month four of your perfect tenant's tenure. The worse is yet to come!

You now have four months' worth of arrears that you are never going to get back in a million years. The dilemma is this… Do you now settle for the fact that if you didn't put them in you would have had a couple of void months anyway, and from now on you are going to be paid direct from the benefit agency? Or do you decide to serve notice on them and start this whole process again, whilst waiting with trepidation to see what state they will leave the property in? You will then have refurbishment costs on top of the arrears as well.

So what do you do? You decide that out of principle you are going to evict them and make them inconvenienced like you have been. You serve them eight weeks' notice as per the legal requirement and it lands on their doorstep. They phone you and start effing and blinding, and saying things like 'Who do you think you effing are? The tap in the bathroom drips and the seal on the bedroom window lets a draught in and there is damp in our bedroom blah blah blah!' All of a sudden because you have threatened them with eviction you are public enemy number one! They shout down the phone, 'You are the worst landlord ever, not doing repairs and the damp is a nightmare and we are going to call environmental in to sort you out!'

That is their cue to start looking for another property – not that they will tell you they are looking. They will just make your life a misery, constantly complaining to you and getting everyone and anyone who will listen at the council to phone you as well to sort out all the problems with your property (which they didn't have before you served notice on them). All the while you are distracted with this, they are out viewing properties, telling letting agents and landlords what a horrible landlord you are and the whole cycle will start again for some other poor landlord who just wants to let his property out!

Recently published statistics from the Ministry of Justice show a big jump in possession claims submitted to court and in court orders subsequently granted to landlords.

Possession orders are up 12% on the previous 12 months, at 36,211, and 70% higher than the 21,352 granted three years ago.

For landlords accepting tenants on local housing allowance, Crisis (the national charity for single homeless people) found that in the two years until the end of 2011, almost 10,000 households approached their council for housing at the end of, or during, their tenancy due to arrears problems, a 42% increase.

Chapter 8

You Couldn't Make It Up! – Real Life Stories

Here are some real life examples of tenants we that have encountered over the years.

A sad story...
My wife phoned a tenant to chase their unpaid rent. Her boyfriend said she was in hospital, and we thought this was one of those who were going to get into arrears – with that old chestnut.

My wife phoned back a week later to ask again where the rent was. The boyfriend told us she had gone into premature labour and he would sort the rent out later that day. Yvonne rang again and he told us that they had had a little girl and everything was fine with the baby. He then told us what I can only call a horrific tale of what his girlfriend had been through. She had had complications and septicaemia had set in somehow. He told us that they had amputated both of her legs below the knee! Now I've heard some whoppers in my time, but I was pretty sure he was telling the truth this time. He then continued to tell Yvonne that his girlfriend still wasn't out of the woods yet. They were going to operate and take her womb away (a hysterectomy). By the way, this girl was only twenty-one years old! Luckily she pulled through, but unfortunately they have now split up and she lives with her mum. The last time we spoke to them, the father of the child (her boyfriend) had custody of the child.

An act of stupidity...

We got a call from a tenant to say that she needed the back and front doors securing due to the fact that she had fallen off some steps trying to reach the key meter to top up the electric. Note – I told her to make sure she got some steps when I checked her into the property!

Anyway, she had tried to balance on a chair and whilst reaching up to the meter she fell and banged her head. Now she wasn't unconscious, but decided to dial 999. The ambulance arrived and the paramedics couldn't get an answer from her. Fearing the worst, they called the police who turned up but still, no answer. So they decided to force entry through the back door, where she was supposedly lying in distress. They managed to break the door locks on the uPVC door, but she was lying behind the door. So instead of asking her to move, they went around the front of the house and kicked that door in as well. So the landlord got a bill of around £950 for two new doors and a fee for the police contractor to board the property up and make it secure, while they took the tenant to the hospital. She was released after a check-up and she phoned us to tell us that we would need two doors fixing. I don't think tenants have the faintest idea what things cost or how it affects landlords. They just want it fixed because it's broken and they think that landlords have an endless pit of money that they can just tap into anytime they need something done! Never mind that it was down to her stupidity that they were damaged in the first place.

The smackhead...

I received a call from a distressed landlord who had a problem. He asked if I could meet him at a mutually convenient place to discuss the matter. He was a teacher so he didn't have a lot of time to discuss the nitty-gritty, but gave me a brief overview of his problem.

Cutting a long story as short as I can, he had put the property on the market with a so-called letting agent who is quite big in the north-east. They had decided to put a tenant into his property on the basis that the negotiator in their office knew his next-door neighbour's son. Because the negotiator knew them, he then decided to let him in the property with no credit check, no references, a £250 deposit and the promise that he would pay the rent.

Needles to say, not only did he not pay the rent, but he decided that he wouldn't leave the property for unpaid rent because his parents had advised him that "he had rights" – sound familiar? We found out later that he was what is affectionately known as a "smackhead" (on drugs) but we will come on to that a bit later. So this was the landlord's problem.

Now obviously the landlord was quite distressed to say the least. Especially as his wife was six months pregnant and didn't need the stress, anxiety and tears that this little smackhead was causing them. The tenant didn't care, because the rent money was going up his nose, in his veins or wherever he decided to shove it.

Now to a novice landlord or investor – or another letting agent, this would be a massive problem. Getting a Section 21 notice served, getting the courts to issue a court order, getting a bailiff to go and evict him. This whole process can take months to get through and costs you money, by the way (at the time of writing this: £175 for initial registration to start the process in court, £250 for a court order, and a further £250 for bailiff service – total £675) – not to mention that your tenant is living rent-free. So if this process takes four months and the rent is £600, before you get the tenant out, you are £3,075 out of pocket. Then when you finally get your property back from the tenant, he has probably trashed it. Even if it is just filthy dirty, needs redecorating and new carpets, that's another £3,000!

But luckily for the landlord, he found our website and called me. I felt heartily sorry for him and his wife and their predicament. I was also disgusted that someone in the same profession as me had put the landlord in this position by their lack of integrity, and their sheer lack of interest when the landlord asked them to help.

I told the landlord to take a deep breath and go home and tell his wife that the problem would be sorted. I told him what was going to happen and when.

I made a phone call to an acquaintance that does a bit of "bailiff" work for us. I gave him the address and he told me when the eviction would be taking place. It wasn't going to court and it was happening three days after my initial consultation with the landlord!

It was a Thursday afternoon and I was busy going about my day. My mobile phone rang and it was my "bailiff" – we'll call him Dirty Den. Den said, 'Can you have a word with the police, they want to speak with you.' I could hardly hear the policeman because I was driving and it was a bad signal, but managed to tell him I would be at the property in ten minutes.

When I arrived, there were two policemen with blue flashing lights, the tenant's mother, the tenant and Den. They were swearing at each other and the police were trying to keep the peace. I introduced myself and they asked on what authority I was trying to evict the tenant. I told him that we had served the tenant with a Section 21 notice to quit the property and that he was obviously going to deny to them that he had been served, as that was what all tenants who don't pay their rent do, I said. So the date had passed and instead of getting a court order we were exercising our right of ownership because he was now trespassing. After a lot of abuse from the tenant and his mother, I told the police that most tenants normally disappear, but on this occasion we would concede that he would only go by force and we weren't going down that route. We would get the court order and come back next week. It was a civil matter, I told them, as Den and I drove off.

That was 1-0 to the tenant and Den and I were boiling up inside because the little waster had got the better of us. 'He must have texted his mother when I let him get dressed and she must have called the police,' Den said. I agreed.

I rang the landlord to give him an update. He asked what we should do next... I told him we would get the relevant paperwork to the court and get a court order, which could take a couple of weeks. He told me that his wife wasn't sleeping, and could we have another go at getting the tenant out before we have to go to court? I admired his spirit and for the sake of his wife we would go again the following day. We had already had the locks changed at the first visit and the tenant didn't have a key. So all we had to do on the second visit was throw him out!

I said I would meet Den this time and we decided to just go in and throw him out, whether he was dressed or not! If his mother was there, we would be able to phone the police ourselves and tell them she was trespassing as long as the son was outside. As luck would have it he was on his own when we barged into his bedroom. He was sitting with his laptop on his knee, his bed was a mattress on the floor and it was like walking into a sauna it was so hot. He had jeans on, no t-shirt, no socks or shoes. Den wasn't going to make the same mistake he made last time and as we burst into the bedroom you should have seen the look on the tenant's face! Den said, 'You didn't expect to see me again did you clever lad?' With that, he just punched the laptop out of his hands and it went flying across the room. He then grabbed hold of the tenant, picked him up and jostled him out onto the landing. Lucky for him, he never fell over the top of the banister and down the stairs. He started shouting like a little girl, 'Can I get my phone, can I get my phone?' 'No you effing can't!' I shouted back at him. Den bustled him out of the door while the tenant tried to reason with him. I had picked up his trainers and a sweatshirt that was lying beside the bed and threw them out of the door. (Obviously if the police did turn up after that we could say he was outside already and we simply locked him out. That wouldn't look true if he was stood outside with jeans and no shirt or shoes!)

Den was busy shouting the odds with the tenant, telling him that he wasn't so clever without his mummy and the police. He also told him that if he came back and bothered the landlord again, either here or at the landlord's home, that we knew where his parents lived!

Meanwhile, we had telephoned the landlord to let him know that the "tenant from hell" was no longer a problem and was out of the property. He said he was on his way to the property to see us. When he arrived, we told him what to say to the police, because no doubt the tenant would be phoning Mummy and she would probably phone the police. The landlord said he would wait around for a bit so we could leave and get on with our day, just in case the tenant tried anything or the police turned up.

I did have other appointments and rang the landlord a couple of hours later to see if everything was okay. He told me that the mother of the tenant had turned up and asked if she could have her son's stuff. I don't know if the landlord had been buoyed by what we had done for him or what, but he said to her, 'Well, you can have his stuff, but I don't want to see you again, and you're not getting this.' With that, he held up the tenant's stash of drugs which were in a clear plastic bag. 'So you can take his belongings and if I never see you again I won't notify the police that I have this bag.' With that, she took his laptop and mobile phone and the rest of his belongings which fitted into a black bin liner. The problem was well and truly sorted!

Now I am not saying that you should all take the law into your own hands, but sometimes you have to fight fire with fire. You have to assess who and what your tenant or tenants are about and make a judgement call. You can either sit around and wait for the courts to give you a piece of paper which, to be honest, is sometimes a complete waste of time and money, or you can take action. Because let's not forget, they are a guest in your house. If it was a hotel they would be turfed out, so what's the difference? All the time they remain in your property they are causing you grief, stress, anxiety and probably sleepless nights. There are so many variables about what the tenants are likely to do to your property, it doesn't bear thinking about. So as soon as you make the decision that you want them out, don't hesitate. Make some phone calls and get it sorted! Below is the testimonial I received from the landlord for services rendered. I haven't given you his name as it isn't relevant. Suffice to say that it is a true story and has been used as an example to prospective landlords looking to use our services for property management.

'I simply cannot recommend Property Finders North East highly enough. I know that this sounds like a line you would read in any good advertisement, but in this case it simply expresses my honest experience of this brilliant company. My wife and I previously used other estate agents, who we found to be universally incompetent at dealing with any property matters beyond putting across a good sales pitch and a load of blather to cover their inaction and regular failings. During a nightmare tenancy situation (through another estate agent), and a time of tears, sleeplessness and on the brink of utter despair, we found Property Finders North East. What a godsend! Decent, honest and hands on people who actually know the practical reality of property letting. Problem sorted. Life returned

to normal. What an unbelievable relief it was to find them. They don't just talk – they do! As I said, I simply cannot recommend Property Finders North East highly enough.'

As thick as mince...

This story has to be told because it is so unbelievable you couldn't make it up. A mother came into the office to ask if she stood as guarantor for her son, would we be able to give him one of our flats to rent? We agreed to let him have it after doing all the necessary checks and paperwork with them.

He moved into a studio flat and his mother helped him move in. He was a bit of a pain in the backside, phoning up every five minutes to ask questions about this and that, but all in all he was harmless.

A few months later, as he was coming to the end of the fixed term of his tenancy, he came in to ask if he could move out as he was going to move into a house with his girlfriend who was already renting another property from us. We agreed, as there had been no rent arrears or issues with him in the studio flat, but we did insist that his mother remained as his guarantor if we added him to the girlfriend's tenancy.

The girlfriend wasn't the sharpest pencil in the box, so they were a perfect match! He moved in with her and whenever they came in with their rent they seemed happy enough.

About a year later, they gave us notice that they were leaving the property. We said we would come and do a pre-check-out inspection to let them know what jobs would need doing to make sure that the property was in a satisfactory condition for their check-out.

Basically it was dirty, so it would need a good clean. The small bedroom would need to be repainted with a neutral colour and the lounge carpet was so dirty I suggested replacing it if it didn't come clean with a carpet cleaner. They told me that it had already been cleaned!

I informed them it would need to be replaced then, and they agreed to it before they handed it back over to us in two weeks' time.

Well, you could have knocked me over with a feather when I turned up to check them out. Their poor attempt at cleaning was totally unsatisfactory. The oven was still dirty, but clean to them! The bedroom I told them to paint back to neutral was bright pink and was patchy, with pink paint all over the edges of the white ceiling! But the biggest shock was the carpet that they had replaced. They had obviously bought a remnant of a carpet and it didn't fit the room! On top of that they had cut "spare bits" into small, one-foot pieces and patched the bare bits of floor. If it wasn't so serious for the landlord, I would have burst out laughing. It was like a patchwork quilt, only the pieces of carpet weren't even stuck together. It was horrible and the funniest part was that they actually thought it would be acceptable. They even had the cheek to get the mother who was guarantor to phone us and argue about the bond, and why weren't they going to get it back? Sad but true!

Two identities...
Steph was one of our early tenants who had just had a boob job. We only knew that because she was so proud of them she told anyone who would listen. She moved into one of our properties and was a pleasant enough girl. A bit ditsy, but bubbly and full of herself. She worked as a beautician for some company, I can't remember where or who they were. She paid her rent on time and kept the townhouse we rented to her in good condition. Nice and clean and a good tenant.

Then one day, Yvonne rang me and asked me to go to the property because Steph's rent was two weeks overdue and she wasn't answering her phone. She wasn't in when I went to the property, so I left a note through her door that she needed to contact the office. It looked pretty much the same as usual and I thought nothing of it. It was unusual for her to be late with her rent, but she may have lost her job or something, I thought.

I was right. She phoned us to say that she had in fact lost her job, but that she would be putting a claim in for housing benefit. No problem, we thought... Wrong! Another week passed by and Yvonne had rung the council to chase up her claim for housing benefit to see how it was progressing and to see how long it would be before the claim was in payment. They told us that they needed more information from the tenant and that her claim would not be progressed until they had the information they required. We tried to phone her on numerous occasions and wrote to her to let her know what was happening. When we finally got hold of her, she said, 'Don't worry, I am working again now and I will pay you some rent next week.' Next week came and went and no money appeared. Yvonne and I were getting annoyed now as she was blatantly telling lies and not co-operating with us at all. I ended up having to go to her property again and threaten her with eviction which she said she didn't want to happen. She said if I followed her to a cashpoint she would withdraw the rent and give it to me. I followed her to a cashpoint and she said it wasn't working. I then had to wait for her to go into the bank and withdraw the money. What a carry on, I thought, but it was the only way we were going to get any money from her. I took the money from her and she promised that the next month's rent would be on time as she would set up a standing order now that she was working again.

Needless to say, this never happened and we had the same problems with her from that day forward. We were spending far too much time on this tenant and she was now still in arrears as she never caught up with the rent she didn't pay when she was out of work. The landlord was obviously frustrated and was always on the phone asking what we were doing to sort it. We agreed with him that it was time to evict her as she was inconsistent and erratic with rent payments and was never ever going to pay the arrears. So we served notice on her to quit the property and gave her the date to hand the property back over to us. The day of her eviction had come and we had agreed with the landlord that we would be changing the locks after she had gone. When we got to the property with the locksmith, we knocked on the door. There was no answer so we let ourselves in. She was already gone! We inspected the property and it wasn't that bad. An old television set and a Freeview box and some other bric-a-brac, but apart from that it wasn't too bad. There was a pile of mail on the floor so she had obviously scarpered a few weeks before the eviction date. I picked up the mail and had a quick look through to see if anything looked like debt letters. Some of them had been opened and just thrown back on the floor, so I had a look at those. They were indeed letters from a debt collection company on behalf of an energy supplier. After looking through the other letters, I noticed that some other letters were in a different name. This wouldn't have surprised me if it was another property, but this property was a new build and she was the first and only tenant that had lived there. If it had been a man's name I would have thought it might be her boyfriend or something, but because it was a female name I thought I would open the letters to see what they were. To my surprise they were energy bills from the same energy company that had sent a debt collection agency after her. I thought they must have sent them to the wrong address. As part of our check-in and check-out process, we inform the energy companies about who moves in and who moves out. I rang them to inform them that Steph had moved out and asked who this other person was at the same address. Had they made a mistake? I explained that she had done a runner and that they should put a trace on her. When they looked into the account and address details they told me that the new tenant "X" had moved in a few months earlier. I told them that she was the only tenant that had ever lived there. After a few moments of silence, the voice on the other end of the phone said that he thought he knew or could guess what had happened. He said that she must have phoned them up a few months earlier pretending to be this new tenant, giving false details as she was in arrears with her energy bills. So she remained in the property, told them that *she* had left, and carried on using the gas and electric in the new name, which was actually her! How do they think of these things? I was gobsmacked.

The tenant who thinks *we* are as thick as mince…
Before we went on holiday, we left instructions with the girls in the office to chase a tenant up who was in arrears. Just before we got back, he rang to say that someone from our office had knocked on his door and demanded £500 from him for rent. He said he had told the mysterious person that he didn't have it, and could they come back tomorrow for it? He never bothered ringing the office to see if we had sent them, and he reckoned he then went out and sold his car so he could pay the mysterious person the rent the next day. He then waited a week to ring us and ask why we had told the council to stop his housing benefit for being in arrears when he had paid someone from our office £500 in cash last week?

Long story short, he phoned me up when I got back from holiday demanding his £500 back that he had paid! I told him that no-one from our office went to see him, so if he had been ripped off by a doorstep conman, then he needed to phone the police. He said, 'Are you calling me an effing liar?' I said, 'No, I am merely stating a fact, that no-one from this office came to collect any money from you. So if you have given someone money and have a receipt with our name on it, you need to phone the police and show them it.' He muttered that he was taking it all the way to the top and promptly hung up. The top of what, I don't know. I am the top!

The next day I got a call from the local police who had been to see the tenant. I explained the conversation I had with the tenant and the policeman said that the tenant also told him that he had a receipt for the money he had paid the mysterious person. He also added that when he went to see the tenant to get a statement that he had lost the receipt. So the policeman and I came to the same conclusion... What a load of bollocks. The policeman told me the case was now closed as far as he was concerned.

So in summary, tenants will make up any cock-and-bull story when they are in arrears. Especially when the council writes to them to say the housing benefit is now being paid to the agent or landlord direct, due to them being in arrears. Expect fireworks if you have an unstable tenant (which you won't find out until it happens to you). Just take a deep breath or tell them you will call them back, and give yourself five minutes to digest what the hell is going on in their little mind!

The lunatic...
One of our contractors was sent to look at a faulty uPVC door that the tenant said he couldn't close properly. It was a Friday morning and he was asked how long it had been like that by the contractor. The reply... 'Oh, a couple of weeks.' The contractor removed the mechanism and needed to take it away so he could get a replacement as the

door mechanism was quite unique. He went back to the property and informed the tenants that he would need to secure the front door (lock it shut) and the part should be in by Monday, and he would return to fix it with the new part first thing on Monday morning. So they would need to use the back door over the weekend. Sound reasonable?

Well, the tenant went berserk with the contractor, effing and blinding and shouting, 'I am not having my effing front door locked, I want it fixed today!' He then rang the office, ranting and raving about the same and I explained to him exactly what the contractor had already told him. That we needed a replacement part and the only way we could secure the property was by locking the door shut until we could fix it. He could still use his back door. The other alternative was to leave it unsecure, which would mean that he would have to stay in all weekend and have the worry that someone might walk in.

He calmed down a bit and told me to send the contractor back to his house and secure the door. I thought that would be the last I would hear of that… WRONG!

Ten minutes later I got the council, the police, the fire brigade and then the Citizens Advice Bureau on the phone. By the time I had spoken to the latter, I was about ready to punch someone. I had to explain the whole story four times and then phone the tenant back to ask what the hell he was playing at. He said he didn't agree with what we had agreed to.

I drove to his house and said, 'If you want this door fixed, that you waited until Friday morning to report, you either want it locked or left open – which is it going to be? The contractor was with me and had been furiously ringing everyone and anyone trying to get the part for this bloody door a bit quicker. He managed to source one as a favour to me and said he would be there at 8 am on Saturday morning to fit it. 'That's the best we can do,' I told the tenant. 'Okay then,' he said. Not a thank you, nothing. It was now 4 pm, so this had been going on all day! The contractor phoned me on Saturday morning and said, 'The lunatic's door is done Dave, have a good weekend!'

Chapter 9

LHA and Universal Credit

Nine out of ten landlords are owed rent by LHA tenants (tenants on benefits) – Tuesday 17th January 2012.

Almost nine out of ten (87%) landlords who accept housing benefit tenants have had problems with rent not being paid on time, with one in ten (11%) saying they have had tenants who stopped paying their rent altogether. Out of all landlords, more than half (59%) stipulate no housing benefit tenants in their advertisements.

The astonishing results emerge from a survey of over 1,000 UK landlords, conducted by a flat and house share website.

The majority of buy-to-let landlords (86%) surveyed were against the change to the benefit system which now automatically pays Local Housing Allowance direct to the tenant.

The change came into force in 2008, and 51% of landlords who take housing benefit tenants said they had mainly experienced rent issues since then.

As part of the survey, landlords were asked why they would not rent out their property to housing benefit tenants. Almost one third (30%) said non-benefit tenants were more reliable, while 47% said they did not want the hassle of dealing with payment problems.

According to the poll, problems caused by benefit tenants included late payments, not paying at all, issues arising from the suspension of benefit payments and damage to the property. More than half (58%) of respondents said they had experienced more than one of these problems.

Three quarters (74%) of those landlords questioned said they would not take a tenant on housing benefit even if the tenant had a guarantor.

One third (34%) of landlords surveyed currently have housing benefit tenants in one or more of their properties, and a further 45% said they had previously taken in this type of tenant.

It's clear from this survey that a reversal of the current system of paying housing benefit to the tenant is desperately needed, and reverting back to the old method of paying landlords or their agents the rental payments directly from the council.

But wait, someone in the government has got an even stupider idea – let's pay the tenants all of their benefits in one lump sum and send the whole of the housing market into complete chaos – let's call it Universal Credit (April 2012).

Universal Credit – bad news for landlords

Introduction

The government have announced new procedures as to how payment will be made under the Universal Credit system when it is rolled out from October 2013 onwards. It means the end of direct payment to landlords for rent as we have known it. The intention for the new procedures will apply across the board to local authority tenants, housing association tenants and tenants in the private rented sector. To some extent it is "work in progress" because the government are conducting pilot schemes in the social sector between April 2012 and June 2013. At the heart of the new procedures is the idea of promoting tenants' abilities to manage their own finances. The key is that there is no longer any back-stop. Landlords will no longer be able to insist on direct payment to the landlord if the tenant is eight weeks or more in arrears.

How the new system will work
As such, the existing system of regulations will disappear. Vitally, there will be no long-stop date.

Decisions as to payment will be made individually on a case-by-case basis according to guidance. All cases will be reviewed from time to time, even if direct payments to landlords are being made.

The Housing Minister has said that the intention is to replicate vulnerability/safe-guarding provisions under the present local housing allowance system but it is clear that a different approach will be taken to decide on those who are vulnerable.

Worryingly, from the landlord's perspective, DWP's stated intention is that only 10% of the caseload should be paid direct to landlords. At the moment for local housing allowance, this could be at least 25% of a council's caseload in the private rented sector and a much higher number in the social sector.

Universal credit will be paid calendar monthly in arrears. The effective date of the claim will fix the first calendar month and the intention is that payment be made seven calendar days after the end of this initial period of one month (brought forward to a working date if it falls on a bank holiday/weekend). Thus, if you have a claim made on the 7th July the first payment should be due on the 14th August and thereafter on the 14th of the month. Assessments will also be made on a calendar monthly basis (rather than weekly, as at present).

The fundamental rule is that there will be one single payment to the claimant, including the housing element. This will be paid into a nominated bank account. This could be at a high street bank or a credit union. For those who do not have a conventional account, payment will be made by the new Simple Money Transmission Service operated for DWP by Citibank. The intention is that these should be made online or by telephone. Where made by telephone, the agent taking the call will complete the details.

Exceptionally, claims can be made face to face at an office or by home visit. Each claim period will be dated from the original claim: e.g. if the claim is made on the 7th of the month, then each subsequent claim period will start on the 7th of the month and the amounts will not be varied, even if individual months are of a different length in terms of the number of days in them. The intention is that to help people budget there will be advice services available and financial products offering automatic payment facilities operating direct debit. Credit unions will no doubt offer this kind of service as at present.

It is proposed that for a minority of claimants alternative systems may be paid other than monthly. However, this sort of arrangement will be time limited.

Third parties will act for those who are incapable of looking after their own affairs e.g. due to mental disorder.

There is no provision for the first payment of benefit to the landlord!

What does this all mean for private rented sector landlords?

Basically, it means you are in the hands of the tenants, who may or may not pay you your rent if they receive Universal Credit! Be afraid, be very afraid, if you currently manage these properties yourself, or have an agent who doesn't know what they are going to do about Universal Credit when it comes into force.

For some landlords, deciding not to take tenants claiming housing benefit is not an option, due to the geographical area or type of housing offered by them. So you will need to find a solution, other than hoping that the tenant will pay you!

Chapter 10

Antisocial Behaviour

One of the big issues we face nowadays is antisocial behaviour. Obviously if you are a homeowner there is very little you can do apart from complain to the council and police and hope that resolves the problem.

It's slightly easier to resolve if you know that the person living in the property is a tenant and is renting, as the landlord or agent can be notified (if you can find out who they are!). Appropriate action can then be taken, as anti-social behavior is a breach of their tenancy agreement – if they have an agent who cares or knows what they are doing.

A recent example of this was when we were notified about one of our tenants. Firstly by the neighbours, then by the police, then by the local authority dealing with it. We wrote to the tenants and spoke to their guarantor, stating that they were in breach of their tenancy agreement. Two warnings later, within weeks of them receiving the first written notice, we served them with a notice (Section 21) to quit the property. Instead of buckling down and behaving, the notice had the opposite affect of what we had intended, which was for them to curb their annoyance to neighbours. So a couple of weeks into their notice, we spoke to the police to see if they were still getting called out to the property in the middle of the night due to the noise, and they confirmed they were. We agreed with the police that we would visit the property and accelerate the eviction with their support and we got the tenants to leave.

Problem sorted. I would just like to add that we inherited this tenant from another agent!

How do we try and prevent it happening in the first place?

1. When we first take the property on, we give our business card to all the surrounding neighbours – so they know who is managing the property. Once the "To Let" board disappears, or if you advertise it yourself, they will only phone the council or police.
2. We speak to the local police beat teams and ask if they are aware of our tenants before they move in.
3. We do a home visit to the potential tenants' current home – to see their lifestyle.
4. We look them up on Google – you will be surprised what you may find.
5. We search their name on www.landlordsbestfriend.co.uk, a FREE website for landlords – set up by Property Finders NE to help private landlords and other letting agents. Because a credit check doesn't tell the whole story!
6. We then do the usual referencing, employment checks and credit searches.

If you choose to use a letting agent and your potential agent only does number 6, then you need another agent! – Please visit www.propertyfindersne.co.uk or call us on 0800 082 8585.

It is vital that we help to stamp out anti-social behavior and the professional scammers from our industry – that includes the rogue letting agents who are only after landlords' property to make a quick buck and don't care about who they put into their properties. There is a whole chapter dedicated to this later in the book (Chapter 13).

Chapter 11

The Councils and their "Help the Homeless" Departments

I would just like to point out that not all councils operate in this way and neither will all tenants they give you be the same as the examples I am going to give you. This chapter is to help you make an informed decision and make sure you are not caught out by the lure of getting a tenant for one of your properties that may be in an area that you struggle to find tenants for.

The council worker will naturally tell you that the person has a sob-story, sorry, a genuine reason for being in the predicament that they are in. They will assure you that you will be paid direct from the benefit agency because their clients are classed as vulnerable tenants. This is the hook that will be music to your ears. You have a property that is always empty and this is your chance to fill it with a tenant who is on benefits and your rent is "guaranteed" because the council will pay you direct. Fantastic? Read on...

Example 1

We took a call from one of our friendly councils who asked us if we would take Susie and Michael who needed somewhere to live. Michael had to cycle five miles to sign on for his benefits and Susie, his girlfriend, was due to have a baby, so they needed somewhere to live. Because the landlord was desperate to fill a property that had been empty for three months we put them into the property. The benefit claim had been submitted by the council and they said we should expect their first payment in about four weeks' time. Happy days, we thought.

A couple of months later, we got a call from a neighbour about the male tenant. He was annoying everyone around him and all the other neighbours since he had moved in, apparently. They had been trying to track us down to complain and had finally got our number from someone who we gave a business card to, as we always do when a tenant moves into one of our properties.

The neighbour told me that the previous night the police were called because the tenant had been trying to break into a house in the neighbourhood. He had been chased to his own house (that we manage) and locked all the doors. Whoever had chased him picked up a brick and promptly threw it through the front bay window. The police were called and there was a right fracas. The police called their contractor and boarded the front window up to secure the property. An hour later, the back window got put out and the police returned again. This time, however, they had been given more information about the tenant of a more serious nature. We were told it was serious enough for them to arrest him by gaining access to the property. The tenant failed to answer the door. As he was already on a tag (unbeknown to us) and was also in breach of his bail conditions, the police decided to gain entry by kicking the door down! Now I am no policeman or brain surgeon, but why the hell didn't they just pull the boards off the front window that was already smashed and climb in and arrest him? So we then got another call to let us know that all this had occurred and that we needed to make sure that the property was made secure – again.

We complained to the police complaints division, on behalf of the landlord, and were told that the police had every right to demolish the door to gain access and that no compensation would be offered to the landlord. The landlord tried to claim on his insurance policy as most policies cover for damage caused by third parties and emergency services. However, because the damage was caused in three separate incidents, they made the landlord do three separate claim forms – even though as far as he was concerned, it all happened on the same night and should have been treated as one claim. Therefore, the insurance company deducted an excess charge from each claim. One window was £200 which was below the excess – nothing due to the landlord! The second window cost £260 so they sent him a cheque for £10. The door and replacement framework cost £650 so they sent a cheque for £400! So what should have been a claim for £1110 with a £250 deduction, leaving the landlord with a bill for £250, ended up costing the landlord £710 and the insurance company £400. (So read your own policy very carefully before renewing or taking out a new one!) Then, to add insult to injury, the insurance company told the landlord that when he comes to renew his policy, because he has had three claims in one year (which should have been one claim) the new excess amount would be going up to £1,000 – in other words don't bother claiming again – ever! I know all these facts to be true – because the landlord was me!

When the truth finally came out in court, the tenant had argued with his girlfriend and she had decided to take her clothes off and parade around the front room (drunk) and naked in front of all the neighbours and children when he went out. That was why the front window was put out. Meanwhile he was out doing a burglary and was nearly caught in the act. The victim of the burglary had chased him to his own house and that was why the back window was put out, and then the police were called!

So we served them notice to quit the property. To add insult to injury, we then received a letter from the council advising us that the housing benefit we were being paid was to be reduced by £40 per month because of a previous debt he owed to another landlord. Again, no mention of any of this when we were offered the tenants in the first place! The whole episode was a disaster from start to finish and we now have an insurance excess of £1,000 on the property.

Example 2

We had another call from a different council who had a lady who was living in a hostel with her children because she had been the victim of a violent relationship. The benefits agency would pay us direct because of her circumstances. We agreed to let her into the property without a bond after discussing it with the landlord.

She was over the moon with us and promised to look after the property and was really thankful for the new home.

A few months went by and we had a phone call to say that there was a problem with the shower. We had it fixed and thought nothing of it after that. A few weeks later she rang the office and spoke to a member of staff like she was a piece of dirt on her shoe. She was insulting her, swearing and being quite rude. When I found out, I rang her and told her that I wasn't impressed with her attitude and swearing at staff. She apologised and said that there was a problem with the shower that hadn't been fixed for weeks. I said if it hadn't been fixed properly the last time, all she had to do was ring us and let us know, instead of waiting weeks and weeks to ring us. She apologised again and that was that.

About a year went by and we got a phone call from her letting us know that she would be leaving the property and was giving us a month's notice. We were quite shocked as this was a lady with no means or ability to pay for a deposit etc. when she came to us.

We made an appointment to do her check out of the

property. (We normally take meter readings, check the inventory to make sure there is no damage and take keys from the tenant.)

I was waiting outside the property for her to arrive when I received a phone call saying that she was in hospital and could not make the appointment. Could we do it next week so she could finish tidying the property and get the rest of her stuff? I said I would ring her back with a new appointment. I had my set of keys so I thought I would check the property over while I was there. When I went inside, it was filthy. The new carpets we had put down before she moved in were covered in food and drink stains and the place was generally in a bad condition.

I rang her and gave her another appointment and told her that I hoped she was going to give the place a good clean throughout as it was filthy. She said she would and would see me next week.

I arrived for a second time at the property and it was exactly the same as the first visit. I rang and texted her to see where she was. No answer. I rang one of our contractors to get the locks changed. She texted me to say that she had a tumour and wasn't able to make it and blah blah blah! I texted her back and basically told her that I thought she was totally out of order after we had helped her in her hour of need and if this is how she repaid people she wouldn't get very far in life. I also told her the locks were changed and if she wanted any of her rubbish she had seven days to make an appointment to get it. We never heard from her again! – until two weeks before Christmas. The cheek of her! She rang to ask if her Christmas decorations were still in the loft. We told her they had been cleared out with all of her rubbish!

Example 3
We had a call from yet another council asking the same

questions and would we be prepared to accept a homeless person? This time he was an ex-offender and had served time for an offence, but due to the fact that he had a support worker and he would be classed as vulnerable, we would get the rent direct and the usual patter. We arranged a viewing and he turned up with his wife and daughter. They all seemed pleasant enough and because he was with his wife and daughter we spoke to them and asked what the situation was. They didn't tell us much but his wife (who was his ex-wife now) said that because of their daughter they had stayed in touch and she had helped him through whatever it was he had been locked up for.

The deposit and all fees were being paid between his family and the council. We arranged a move-in date and they moved all of his furniture in.

Only a week later, we received a call from a neighbour asking who this guy was that had moved in. They had heard shouting in the street and the next thing they heard was a car window being smashed. We phoned the support worker and asked what he had been up to. We didn't get to speak to the lady who had originally brought him to the property as it was her day off. But the lady on the end of the phone said, 'I will get sacked if I tell you what he was in prison for, but I can tell you that he was in the paper seven years ago regarding his court case.' With that, she promptly hung up without giving her name.

We immediately did a search on the internet for that period to see what his name search brought up... He was a paedophile! He had molested young girls. We phoned the council the next day and asked to speak to the support worker in charge and promptly told her that we needed him out of the property. They said that because someone had already found out where he was living they were moving him out anyway. They even had the cheek to ask if they could have his deposit back, which we obviously refused.

It was this particular case which prompted us to do an internet search on every applicant that we process, and it was the very last time that we took anyone in from the homeless section of the council. We do work with other organisations where they actually take an interest in the person they are trying to help. Unlike the councils whose names I won't mention, who just wanted to get people off their books so they could say they were doing a good job!

So my advice to you is this. If you are going to take anyone from the council, make sure you do your due diligence on the applicant. Ask the right questions that they WILL be able to answer:

Q: Have they got any arrears from a previous tenancy that may affect their claim on my house?

Q: Have they been convicted of a serious crime, or if you can't tell me that, what risk factor are they? High or low risk?

Q: Is there anything I should know about this tenant?

Q: Would you put them in one of your houses if one was available?

Chapter 12

Landlord's Best Friend – A FREE Website for Landlords

As you have read, we have been through quite a lot since we started in property. We have made loads of mistakes, some of which have cost us money and some that haven't. But the main thing that it boils down to is the quality of the tenant and the whole vetting process in the first place. Don't be suckered in by all the sob stories and promises of building a bond up once they are in the property. Don't listen to someone who tells you they are thirty-five years old with three kids that swear they have lived at home with their mum for three years. They (tenants) will think of anything you will want to hear to get into your property. Their mother, brother, aunty, uncle, grandma or cousin has just died and they were living with them, but now the house is gone and they need somewhere to live. Some were born to lie and scam and trash as many properties as they can get into, to get their housing benefit. They will lie and lie until they actually believe their own lies! Again, I am not talking about the honest hardworking tenants, or the honest tenants that claim housing benefit who just get on with it and pay their rent. I am talking about the minority who are growing in their numbers, who are up to no good and we need to make sure they are driven out of the private rented sector!

People are asking why Landlord's Best Friend (LBF) is different to every other referencing site on the internet. Landlord's Best Friend is not about referencing against the information a tenant gives you, it is about the information that they don't give you! Landlord's Best Friend gives landlords the chance to protect their investment from scammers, con artists and fraudsters. Tenants aren't going to give you their last landlord's if they know they have either ripped them off or damaged/destroyed their property. It is time to get landlords working together towards a common goal of weeding out the dodgy tenants, and giving good, honest, trustworthy tenants the chance to live in a property that otherwise wouldn't be available.

We know some tenants just want somewhere nice to live and pay their rent on time and look after the property they call home. The website will not affect them whatsoever. It's for the minority of tenants who give landlords sleepless nights, cost them money and in some cases force them into bankruptcy!

That is why passing on information to other landlords and letting agents and getting them to join the LBF family is our daily quest; spreading the word will strengthen the LBF family. Every time a member tells someone and they become a member, another friend is added and slowly but surely the LBF family will cover the whole country. One of the strengths of any family is communication. If you had a great meal at a restaurant you would tell your family and friends. If you saw a great movie you would tell your family and friends. So if you had a tenant that left you in arrears, destroyed your property that you have spent your hard-earned cash on, and then threatened you when you had the "audacity" to take back possession of your property, then why wouldn't you tell your family and friends? Information that is passed amongst landlords and agents through LBF will protect landlords against enemies and foes.

Although Landlord's Best Friend cannot change the law, the cheats, the con artists and scammers who destroy our property and steal our rent, we can make sure it doesn't happen to a member of our family's properties. So, honest tenants have nothing to fear from our family. But the "dodgy tenants" will either have to toe the line, go to the council (who don't have enough properties) or simply become homeless.

Tell every landlord and letting agent you know about this website… IT'S FREE… and the more people you tell… the more people register… the more protection it gives YOU! We are passionate about protecting landlords – because we are landlords ourselves. We have suffered what you have suffered… and it's painful. How much did one bad tenant cost you? Don't let these tenants do it to someone else. Go to the website and register – IT'S FREE – FOREVER – unlike some sites which purport to be free but only for a limited period. We will never charge anyone to use this site, otherwise why would you join or recommend us? We do this because it helps us personally and helps our business. So why would we start charging? It's a necessary business expense that actually saves us money in the long run.

At the last time of looking www.landlordsbestfriend.co.uk was getting 1021 monthly visitors. So there is obviously a need by the private rented sector and landlords who are looking for this type of service.

It is not a name and shame website. It is set up in such a way that it will merely let you know who the tenants' previous landlord was.

Chapter 13

Beware of the Rogue Letting Agents

Most property management companies and letting agents are good, honest, decent people who offer a service to landlords that don't have the experience, time or inclination to manage their own properties themselves. Landlords put their trust in them because they just want an armchair investment which gives them a decent return. All they ask for is a monthly statement, a monthly payment and a return phone call if they need something. They don't want the day-to-day dealings with tenants, contractors, housing benefit queries, utility companies, neighbour complaints about their tenants etc. So they try and do their due diligence and pick an agent or company they think they can trust. Being landlords ourselves, we have done the very same thing – had a look on Rightmove, made a few phone calls, asked how much they charge and plucked one out of the air! Simple! BIG mistake, unless you are lucky. But in this business, you need to be more than lucky, you need to be careful.

Unfortunately there are no real checks done on people who decide to set up a letting agency or property management company. Just like any other self-employed business, once they have premises (or not) and a company telephone number, they are good to go. As far as I am concerned, all letting agents should be regulated in much the same way as mortgage advisors. Letting agents will handle more cash and landlords' money than the average business – something I had not fully appreciated until we grew to the size we are now. That is probably why this business attracts the wrong sort of people sometimes. Some of our landlords' properties are also in licenced areas. This means that there are extra costs involved as these schemes are normally run by the government and the local councils. What it means to you as a landlord is that you or the managing agent needs to be fully vetted, to make sure that you or your agent are a fit and proper person to hold the licence. They do police checks, and vet you as if you were applying for a job. So my question to the government is, "Why can't you do this for all landlords and letting agents?" It would make the industry a whole lot safer for tenants and landlords. There are a lot of other things to take into consideration with regard to this question, but there definitely needs to be *some* regulation for letting agents in particular. Anyway, I will get off my soapbox now. Let's continue.

I will lay a few numbers on you, then it might actually make you realise the full potential of buy-to-let if you are serious about building a property portfolio for yourself. It will also help you understand why there are so many self-made millionaires out there as a direct result of owning property. It will also give you an idea of why there are some characters out there that see it as a "get-rich-quick-on-other-people's-property-scheme". The undesirables of the industry should be regulated so we can rid the industry of them before they can get a chance to set up in the first place.

Take a small business with only 100 properties with an average rent of £500 coming into their business from tenants.

That equates to £50,000 per calendar month which equals £600,000 per annum. You can see from those numbers why people get into buy-to-let and/or property management. If it's done right, it can be big business. If you have enough capital yourself to build a decent property portfolio it can give you a very serious income and help you retire comfortably well-off.

Now most agents only charge 10% management fees, but it's not what they make for themselves that appeals to the rogue letting agents, it's the potential of all that money coming into their bank account every month that appeals to them!

I know of two men who set up a letting agency who couldn't stand up straight if their lives depended on it. Yes, I mean they were crooked! What could I do? I tried to warn landlords to avoid them and I couldn't go to the police because they hadn't actually committed a crime – YET! But I knew in my own heart what they were going to do. Anyone that knew them knew it would happen, and sure enough two and a half years later, shock horror, they had gone bust – taking all the landlords' rent and tenants' deposits with them!

We started out as novices just like you. One property, one tenant, one agent. No problem. But then as your portfolio grows, the properties may not be in the same area or even the same part of the country, so you might need more than one agent.

Yvonne and I had got to the stage where we had about five properties with one agent. Every month we had to ring and ask where the monthly statement was and when we could expect the rent. It might sound familiar if you already have an agent acting for you. Every month we couldn't work out how much we were actually going to receive, and didn't have the statement, so we couldn't decipher what was going on. In the end we just gave up and told the agent we were withdrawing the properties and would manage them ourselves. This was when we found out what was really going on…

After getting all the files and tenant contact details, we

rang the tenants and made appointments to go and visit them all. One by one, they told us how every time they reported a repair, they were given the same answer. 'We will ask the landlord and get back to you.' In the end they had given up and either done the repair themselves or just left it broken or in disrepair. One of the tenants told us that the toilet was cracked and it needed replacing. The joke of it was that when we asked if he knew a local plumber he said, 'I am a plumber.' So we got him to fix it and send us an invoice. Job done.

It was from that moment that we decided to do our own property management.

It still amazes me that landlords who receive the same sort of service are scared to change managing agents. They put up with this appalling service month after month and never leave. Why? We get numerous phone calls from landlords telling us how bad their current agent is. They ask all the right questions of us, and tell us they are going to serve notice on their current agent. When we don't hear from them we follow it up with a courtesy phone call and hear the same thing over and over again 'We decided to give them another chance.' Why? Because the agent gave them the same sales pitch they did on day one! Or maybe because they just couldn't be bothered with all the hassle! If they asked their current agent all the questions they asked us, they probably wouldn't have gone with them in the first place!

Those same landlords ring us back a few months later and tell us their current agent has gone bust, and could we help them out? Yes we can, but it would have been a whole lot easier if we had all the files, the deposits etc. And just in case you don't know, if an agent disappears with your tenants' bond money, YOU, the landlord, are liable in certain circumstances to cover it, if and when a tenant ever leaves your property. So you had better make sure your agent has put the deposits in one of the tenancy deposit schemes.

The other popular thing that I have heard that the rogue letting agents do, is the fictitious work on your property. If their cashflow is looking a bit poor one month they will just type out a load of invoices for work that has never been done. Send them off to the individual landlords, deduct the money from the rent, and hey presto they have just made themselves a couple of thousand pounds (depending on how many properties they manage).

I know of one agent that was bragging to me that he could make £6,000 per month from repairs because he just invoiced his landlords on different months for different repairs. These are the sorts of things that make my blood boil! Again, I will repeat that most agents *don't* do this. It's the minority that gets away with it until they are caught. Then they simply close up shop and tell everyone their hard luck stories about bad tenants and bad landlords and how it made them "go under"(bankrupt). When in reality they have just mismanaged the whole thing, ripped a few landlords off, and when it all came on top of them they just decided to close the doors and switch their mobile phones off. They don't care about the fallout and the complete mess it leaves both the tenants and the landlords in.

First of all, you need to make sure that your agent gives you a contract in the first place. Make sure there is a provision in the contract relating to minor works and major works. Our contract, for example, says that we have the landlords' authority to carry out repairs up to the value of £150 plus VAT. This enables us to instruct contractors for emergency callouts in the event of boiler breakdowns or water leaks or other minor repairs. That way we don't have to ring the landlord for every little repair. For anything over and above that, we contact the landlord for authorization. Obviously there are going to be anomalies, but they are few and far between. We will always contact the landlord if the amount is over £150. If it is a real emergency and the landlord doesn't get back to us quick enough, then obviously we need to get it sorted.

I will give you a quick example of this. It was early December a couple of years ago and I was in London for the weekend with my wife Yvonne. It was that year when the country was absolutely frozen. The north-east was being hit by really heavy snowfall. The phone rang at about 5 pm on the Friday afternoon. Yvonne and I had just sat down for a cup of coffee in a local coffee shop. It was one of our landlords' tenants informing us that a gas fitter had been to their house to try and fix the boiler. He was unable to fix it and told them it needed a part. With that, he promptly left telling them he would get in touch with us and sort it out next week! Like I said, it was absolutely freezing and my first thought was that they would need some type of heating over the weekend. I rang one of our contractors and our office and organised for three electric heaters to be delivered to them. It was about an hour and a half round trip from our office to the property in four inches of snow. But the tenants rang us back to thank us for our concern and expressed their appreciation for what we had done. We tried to contact the landlord but as he lived in Australia there was a slight problem with time difference. Yvonne and I decided between us that it was time to replace the boiler, which had to be ordered. It was going to take a couple of days to get one fitted, but the tenants were quite happy to wait as they had heaters and an electric shower. The landlord eventually contacted us and it was another emergency dealt with.

Do you think the rogue agent would have done what we did? Probably not! The tenant would have got an answer machine and been left in the lurch to freeze.

You have to be prepared for everything and anything in the property game.

So what are the warning signs when you are in the hands of a rogue letting agent?

You don't get your monthly statements unless you ring up for them. When you do ring, you can never get through. When you do eventually get through to someone, they take a message and tell you that someone will get back to you. It never happens! You email them and ring them and go through the whole process again. Then you finally get hold of the person you were trying to speak to – because they were never going to ring *you*. They tell you the statement and cheque are in the post. You believe them and hang up. It finally arrives two weeks later. When you look at it you realise it is not only wrong, but the next payment is now due and you have to start the whole process again!

Communication is the key to any effective business. You should expect no less from your letting agent or property management company. If they can't get the statements and/or the rent to you on a regular basis without the need for you chasing it up every month, then you have to ask yourself, what sort of systems they have? And why is it so haphazard? Also, if they can't get something as simple as the rent and the statements to you, or even effectively deal with your enquiry, then what chance do you think the tenants have got of getting any repairs reported? Let alone repaired? You should be very concerned if this happens to you. Don't let the agents fob you off. Serve notice on them that you will be removing the property from them and get the files and tenant contact details from them as soon as possible. Make sure you have another agent ready and waiting to take over (after doing your due diligence).

If the communication is rubbish, then it stands to reason that everything else under their control will be. Don't wait for them to send the files either. Write to your tenants immediately and tell them to cease payments to the letting agent with immediate effect. Ask them to contact you and discuss with them how and when they pay their rent. If they are on benefits, ask which housing benefits office they deal with and make sure you get the housing benefit suspended. YOU own the property, not the letting agent. Explain to the housing benefit officer what problems you have been encountering (briefly) and they will be quite happy to follow your instructions. Make sure you keep your tenants notified though, as failure to communicate with them could end up with them leaving because they don't like not knowing – because the housing benefit office will write to them to tell them their housing benefit has been suspended. So always make contact with the tenant before you do anything. The last thing you want is an angry tenant – especially if you live hundreds of miles away!

Another thing the rogue letting agents do is pass on their dodgy tenants. How do they do that? I hear you ask. Well, the first thing they do is serve notice on their tenant whom they have decided to evict. They will be ever so nice to the tenant so they can get rid of a problem. They will normally tell the tenant that the landlord has decided to sell the property, so they are giving them eight weeks to find somewhere else to live. If however they find somewhere sooner than that, then they will be happy for the tenant to move out straight away, and they will provide them with a glowing reference. Most tenants won't query their motives (especially if they know they have been the worst tenants in the world). The tenant will normally tell *you* at your first meeting that the landlord or agent have been a nightmare and they wouldn't do any repairs, so they are glad to be moving. If they say any of the aforementioned, be afraid, be very afraid! Just go along with what they have told you but be extra vigilant when you do your background checks. Ask for bank statements showing their rent payments or a rent book if they paid in cash. Also make sure you do a home visit. The best way to find out about their lifestyle is to see them in their own habitat. Arrange a mutually convenient date with them in about a week or so, and let them know it's just a part of your process – because chances are that no-one else will ever have done that to them. They won't refuse if they want *your* property. You will have the address and tell them it is the last thing you will do. First of all, you will need to do a credit reference and do background checks on them with the council and the police. Also check that they are not registered on www.landlordsbestfriend.co.uk. If they ask why you do that, you simply inform them that it's to make sure they have not been involved in any antisocial behaviour or disputes with neighbours.

Trust me, those questions will put the fear of God into them if they are lying or have been tenants from hell. So imparting this information with them should have the desired effect. They will either come clean about why they are moving or they will say it's fine and you will never hear from them again! Either way, it will save you some time.

If they say that it's fine for you to do all those checks, then don't be fooled into NOT doing the home visit. In fact, make sure you do a drive-by the house a few days before the appointment. I would also go past the house in the early evening, just after it's dark, to see if there is any noise etc. You may see a different picture at night! If it looks like the tenants are in and it looks scruffy and bedraggled, then stop and knock on the door. Tell them you were just passing and thought you would save them some time. Do they mind if you come in? Always ask if you can use the toilet and have a look around. This impromptu visit should tell you all you need to know about their lifestyle. If it is filthy dirty and they apologise for the mess as they weren't expecting you – who cares! Most people have a slightly untidy house if they aren't expecting company. But there is no excuse for filth. That's one thing they can't hide. Kids' toys and clothes lying around is one thing, but real dirt and grime is another! Walk away and thank them for their time. Send them a rejection letter as soon as you get home!

It may seem like a lot to do for one potential tenant, but believe me, it will be well worth it in the long run. Bad tenants can cost you more than just money. As mentioned in an earlier chapter, it can save you thousands of pounds and the anguish, heartache and stress of what tenants can potentially do to your property.

Chapter 14

The Tax Man

In May 2010, I received a letter in the post from HMRC requesting a meeting with us and our accountant. It was just regarding a tax return for the previous year and "was nothing to worry about" according to our accountant.

The meeting – the tax man and his sidekick turned up late and asked if we had received an agenda. Our accountant informed them that we hadn't so they handed us all a piece of paper which was a letter about the meeting. With hindsight we should never have taken the meeting and adjourned it to another day, as we were ill-prepared (obviously, having no agenda). Basically we were hijacked by them and they were carrying out a fact-finding mission about personal expenditure and liabilities etc. The accountant was as much in a state of shock as we were, I think. We had a recess and the accountant asked us, 'How do you think it is going?' We replied in the negative and he agreed. We adjourned the meeting and that's when the fun really started. The tax man got out his briefcase and said that because he was unhappy with some of our answers he was going to open up a full enquiry into our personal tax returns for the last few years! Our hearts sank as he issued us with the relevant paperwork. He said they would be in touch and that was that. We were going to have our first compliance check. Now that doesn't sound too bad, does it? Let me tell you that it doesn't matter what they call it, it's a tax investigation from people who don't care how much pain it is going to cause you! They don't care how many sleepless nights you are going to have or how many times you tell them "you can't find it" (an invoice or piece of requested information). You are guilty until proven innocent!

After the meeting, I thought I had better do a bit of research on tax investigations. When I searched on the internet I was flabbergasted and dismayed at all of the horror stories about HMRC – some telling stories of investigations that have gone on for six years!

We tried to kid ourselves that we weren't that concerned, but after reading the horror stories on the internet and how they (HMRC) were specifically targeting landlords and anyone involved in property, the sleepless nights started. The article below is just one of the more recent stories taken from the internet.

The taxman will be launching HMRC tax enquiries and tax investigations into the tax affairs of "Buy-to-Let" landlords who do not pay the right amount of tax; HMRC's new tax evasion taskforce will focus on property rentals in London, Yorkshire, East Anglia and the North East of England.

But in reality, when they have finished in these areas they will move on to their next victims. So expect a visit in the very near future if you have any property other than your main residence. This is the government's idea of helping the country out of recession – targeting the very people they profess to be trying to help. Small businesses.

In their war on tax evasion, HM Revenue and Customs have identified UK property rental "hotspots" that will be targeted in their bid raise an additional £7bn per year by 2014/2015 from tax evasion, tax avoidance and tax fraud. In 2012, HMRC recovered £50m from similar task forces;

the most recent HMRC tax amnesty opportunity being available to online traders.

> **'We have made it clear that we will not tolerate tax evasion – everyone needs to pay the taxes they owe in full. We are determined to crack down on the minority who choose to break the rules. It is not fair, that at a time when most hard-working people are paying the right tax, others are trying to get out of paying what they should. This is not an empty threat – HMRC can and will track you down if you choose to break the rules,' announced David Guake, the Exchequer Secretary to the treasury, in HM Revenue and Custom's press release on 31 May 2012.**

Due to articles like the ones above, I decided that I had better do some research on tax investigations and what they can reasonably ask for and what they can't.

I was shocked to find out that once they have opened up a full-blown investigation into your tax affairs they can pretty much ask for anything. We had to provide bank statements, credit card statements, receipts and invoices for things we had bought or paid for four or five years previously!

The five-page document the tax man sent us was even asking for proof that a cheque my mother gave me for a holiday was in fact from her. Yvonne and I had paid for a holiday and my mother gave us a cheque to cover her portion. Unfortunately my mother died in May 2010 so I wasn't about to start requesting copies of cheques from my deceased mother's bank account! Because I declined to offer up this evidence, it was going to be classed as undeclared income.

If that example wasn't shocking enough for you, how

about this one? Yvonne likes a game of bingo now and again and she had a small win of about £500. Obviously not wanting to leave that sort of cash lying around the house, she paid it into our bank account. When the tax man asked where the money came from, we told him. Because we couldn't provide proof of where it came from… you guessed it – undeclared income that we were going to be taxed on! Oh, and penalties for not declaring it and interest on the whole amount!

Needless to say, these are the sort of things that make your blood boil and get you depressed during the whole process. All the while you are thinking, 'Why us?' You just have to get on with it and try and concentrate on your day job as well. Because this is not the sort of thing you share with anybody. You certainly can't do any of it during the day as you have to get on with earning the money that the tax man wants you to pay tax on! So after your 8-12 hour day at the office, you go home, have your tea, and instead of going to the gym or watching the television, you get all the paperwork down from the loft and start doing some more work for the tax man. Let's not forget there is a deadline every time he writes to you. Depending on how many holes he has picked out of the last lot of information you sent him, he will give you between thirty and forty-five days to reply. So it's not as if you can just forget about it. The more information you send him, it seems, the more questions come flying back at you thirty days later!

So this ping-pong-letter sending went on for months and months. The longer it went on, the angrier and more frustrated I got. Yvonne and I argued sometimes and it really affected our relationship. In her words, we aren't the happy-go-lucky people we were before this investigation. Luckily we had, and still have, a strong relationship, so we got on with it, but I can honestly say that I wouldn't wish an investigation of this type on anybody. It consumes your life, your every waking moment and self-doubt starts to creep in. You keep telling yourself that you have nothing to hide and everything will be alright, but then another brown envelope hits the doormat and there are another raft of questions that need answers.

It got to the point that I believed that the tax man just wouldn't quit until he found something significant to hang on us. So I decided to call the accountant and ask for a meeting with the tax man as it was getting ridiculous. Not to mention that we were at the end of our tether.

The tax man told my accountant that if he was to agree to a meeting he would be expecting an offer if we wanted the investigation to come to an end! It was like music to my ears – he actually wanted an offer to bring the investigation to a conclusion!

The accountant agreed and the date was set for about a fortnight later. This time I was going to be prepared! There was no way I would be leaving that meeting without knowing that it was over. It was July 2012 – two years and two months after the investigation started!

I was going to prepare myself this time and be armed and dangerous, I told Yvonne. I read just about the whole of the tax man's own bible – their own guidance notes and information relating to compliance checks. It made interesting reading and I felt a lot more confident having read it. I highlighted every paragraph that I thought was relevant to the meeting or that I might need and put tabs on each page that I had highlighted. I felt like a solicitor preparing for a court battle.

I had various other things prepared that had been asked for but not submitted; I had them to hand just in case they were needed. Like I said before, I wasn't coming out of that meeting unless we had reached an agreement!

I also prepared an opening statement which I felt was necessary to somehow humanise the whole procedure and to give our perspective on how we felt the compliance check had been going, offering an opinion on what it meant for us and how we had been dealt with thus far by HMRC. I read it aloud to the tax man and his sidekick before any discussions took place. I haven't included the whole thing as it was a four or five page document, but below is a summary which I will share with you in case you ever get a compliance check of your own. My accountant and my solicitor thought it was a good idea. I will let you read it for yourself and let you know at the end whether or not it was a good idea!

Summary of my opening statement to HMRC

We have fully co-operated with the compliance team thus far. Not only have we co-operated (by your own admission – letter dated 15/3/12) we have supplied information above and beyond what has been asked for. Some of which you have used against us, which should tell you that we have never tried to be evasive in our dealings with you. To the contrary, we took on board what the "HMRC guidance to staff on human rights & penalties" states –

'We will take into account in calculating the amount of the penalty the extent to which you have been helpful and have freely and fully volunteered any information about income or gains which were omitted or understated.'

We have admitted to things we have done wrong and tried to be as honest as we can. Yes, we agree, we shouldn't have done them, but due to our own naivety and trying to survive whilst growing the business, we did what we thought was right at that time.

We understand that because of the recession,

your department is under enormous pressure to deliver results and we fully understand the reasons why, but we have not used tax avoidance schemes like celebrities, doctors and dentists as highlighted in the national media this week; we have simply made some mistakes.

Let us also not forget that we have set up our business and bought most of our own portfolio in the toughest of economic times. A worldwide recession, not just here in the north east and UK.

We have recently taken over another failing letting agents'clients. Our turnover has increased as a result of this takeover and our VAT bill for the last quarter was in excess of £7,000, so if that continues, we will make HMRC £28,000 in VAT alone in the next twelve months.

While we understand we will have unpaid tax and penalties to pay, surely it is not in the taxpayers' or public interest to make the penalties so severe that it makes five people unemployed with no further income going into the government coffers to help us all recover from this recession. Our understanding of the remit of the compliance team is to help businesses get their systems in order so they pay the correct tax going forward – not to make them bankrupt.

We cannot undo the past, but we can affect the future. Our systems, training and understanding of what we are supposed to do can only get better, armed with the knowledge of this compliance check, which goes hand in hand with HMRC's own litigation and settlement strategy. Please allow us the opportunity to do this. We are not criminals or scammers and offer an honest, ethical service to our clients. We hope after hearing this statement you will realise that we are in this for the long term and not just trying to make a quick buck by avoiding taxes and disappearing into the night. We understand that we are all in this together (the government and the tax-paying public) and hope we can move to bring this enquiry to a swift and amicable conclusion, so it is a win-win for the compliance team, the taxpayer and ourselves.

Thank you for allowing us to read this.

Dave & Yvonne Hall

After reading my opening statement to the tax man and his sidekick, it set the tone for the whole meeting. I think they understood that we wanted it over as much as they did. The meeting went well and we argued about various issues and agreed on some others.

We asked them what sort of figure they had in mind to bring this to a conclusion. We had some figures in our own minds which Yvonne and I had agreed on the night before. If it was going to be a win-win for both sides, then we knew we wouldn't come away with our bottom figure. But we did eventually come to a mutually agreeable figure. We shook hands with the tax man and his side kick and he said, 'That's it, it's over.' Like it was just another day at the office. Which for them it was.

So was my opening statement a good idea? I will never know. All I do know is that we achieved our objective. We brought the investigation to an end. We had our lives back. It was the best feeling in the world. Yvonne and I went home and opened a bottle of wine.

All we had to do now was get up in the morning…

I hope you have enjoyed reading this book. The last bit of advice I will give you is this:

Live life to the full. Take action. Love those who are close to you as if it is your last day on the planet. Make hay while the sun shines and save a bit for your retirement. You never know what's around the corner.

Best wishes,

Dave Hall

Chapter 15

Some Useful Websites

Residential Landlords Association
Represents the interest of private residential landlords in the UK.
    www.rla.org.uk

National Landlords Association
Represents the interest of private residential landlords in the UK.
    www.landlords.org.uk

The Guild of Professional Estate Agents
A national network of carefully selected independent estate agents working together to ensure a "best in class" service to the public in the UK.
    www.guildproperty.co.uk

Free UK Sold House Prices – Nethouseprices.com
Check how much properties were sold for before you buy. No need to register.
    www.nethouseprices.com

Council Tax : Directgov
Find out about Council Tax, including how to pay your bill, details of discounts and exemptions
    www.direct.gov.uk

Rightmove

Search over a million properties for sale and to rent from the top estate agents and developers in the UK

www.rightmove.co.uk

Property Finders North East

A lettings and property management agent. Covering the whole of the North East of England, UK

www.propertyfindersne.co.uk

Landlord's Best Friend

Landlords Best Friend is a FREE list/register/database site for landlords wishing to report bad tenants. Use this site in conjunction with your other vetting procedures. A credit report doesn't tell the whole story!

www.landlordsbestfriend.co.uk